Be Still…

A daily devotional for your quiet time with God

Dale Tavares

Parson's Porch Books

Be Still…A daily devotional for your quiet time with God
ISBN: Softcover 978-1-960326-62-1

Copyright © 2024 by Dale Tavares

Parson's Porch Books is an imprint of Parson's Porch *&* Company (PP*&*C) in Cleveland, Tennessee. PP*&*C is a self-funded charity which earns money by publishing books of noted authors, representing all genres. Its face and voice is **David Russell Tullock** who you can contact at: dtullock@parsonsporch.com.

Parson's Porch *&* Company *turns books into bread & milk* by sharing its profits with the poor.

Be Still...

This book is dedicated to my family and friends. Thanks so much for your support.

I want to say a special thank you to my husband, Danny, for all your support and love throughout all these years. You are still the only one for me! -D

Preface

I hope this book helps to enhance your alone time with God.

Remember a conversation is two ways- talking and listening.

Pour out your heart to God, but also listen to hear his voice.

Study God's word. Remember any devotional book should be used with your Bible, not as a replacement for it.

Now, find a quiet place.

"Be still and know that I am God: I will be exalted among the heathen, I will be exalted in the earth." - Psalms 46:10

January 1

<u>You are it</u>

Remember, during this time of year, many people start making resolutions. Improving yourself is always good. But keep in mind; you are more than your pant size or how fast you can run. God has a mission specific for you. There is no backup plan. No pinch hitters. Only you can do what He has in mind for you to do. Do you know what your mission is? If not, might I suggest quiet time set aside for just you and God? Listen. God is speaking. It is up to us to hear what He is saying to us. Time alone in His presence is what allows us to hear Him more closely.

"A man's heart deviseth his way: but the Lord directeth his steps"- Proverbs 16:9

"For as the rain cometh down, and the snow from heaven, and returneth not thither, but watereth the earth, and maketh it bring forth and bud, that it may give seed to the sower, and bread to the eater: So shall my word be that goeth forth out of my mouth: it shall not return unto me void, but shall accomplish that which I please, and it shall prosper In the thing whereto I sent it. " Isaiah 55:10-11

January 2

<u>Be Still</u>

Stillness is described as the absence of noise and movement. We all rush around so much these days and even when alone in our cars we have the radio, or are listening to podcasts or are talking on our phones headed from one thing to another. We don't get much stillness unless it is deliberate.

I love that stillness is not just about movement but is without noise too. Sometimes quietness gets more attention than noise.

When I was a preschool teacher and the kids were super loud and I wanted them to listen, I didn't raise my voice louder than them. I whispered. Something about that calmed them. I think maybe because secrets are usually whispered. It makes things seem more important if said softly. I feel like God waits till we are still and then He speaks to us the loudest. Maybe He isn't speaking loud with sound but with the most profound things of our lives.

Science tells us that stillness regenerates our brains. Silence relieves stress and tension and helps us to gain perspective.

I think this might be once that the Bible and science agree. Being still is powerful! I would challenge you to just pick a time of the day that works best for you and just be still. Use this time to go into God's word and really listen. Not thinking about the things on your list for the day. Not wondering what you will make for breakfast or dinner. Just be still in His presence. It will make your "to do" list a lot more do-able

"Be still, and know that I am God: I will be exalted among the heathen, I will be exalted in the earth." - Psalms 46:10

January 3

Proximity to God

We have all heard that going to church will not save you. Also, you might have heard that being around or near Christians, will not make you a Christian. Both these statements are true. I like to use an analogy about my plants to better explain this. I have several plants in my kitchen window near my sink. They are very close to a source of water. But, those plants, even with their proximity to a water source, if never watered, will sit there and dry up and die. Even though they are so close to the kitchen sink, without access to the water it doesn't matter. The same is with us. We have to have a relationship to the "living water" or we will wither and dry up. We can't just know "about him". Or be close to those that have a relationship and think that will water our soul. Think about Judas. Judas hung out with Jesus daily. Yet he still betrayed Him.

"In the last day, that great day of the feast, Jesus stood and cried, saying if any man thirst, let him come unto me, and drink. He that believeth on me, as the scripture hath said, out of his belly shall flow rivers of living water."- John 7:37-38

"For my people have committed two evils; they have forsaken me the fountain of living waters, and hewed them out cisterns, broken cisterns, that can hold no water." - Jeremiah 2:13

January 4

Through the wilderness

Being a Christian doesn't mean life will always be rosy and filled with sunshine and rainbows. Sometimes it is quite different.

God doesn't magically make all our problems go away. But He does promise that He will be there with you through them.

Like the Israelites who wandered in the wilderness for 40 years, we need to learn to trust God more than man. Every day God provided the manna for them for that day- but they had to trust Him, daily. They had to learn that God will make a way even where it seems impossible. God will fight for you. (I would encourage you to read whole chapter of Exodus to understand the full story).

We can learn a lot from the Israelites. They witnessed the 10 plagues, parting of the Red Sea, God gave the Israelites food and even water from a rock and yet they still doubted God. He did so much for them, yet they murmured and complained.

God's timeline is not necessarily the same as ours. But His plans are always better.

It is so very easy for us to forget all our blessings and all the times that God has come through for us. Our human minds only tend to remember the troubles. We forget all the times when God provided when there was no other way. I suggest you start a journal of all the times God showed up for you. It will help you remember. We all need to be reminded. In the Bible God commanded the Israelites to cross the Jordan River which he stopped miraculously and then after they crossed He told Joshua to take a member from each tribe to grab a stone and lay them down so that when future generations asked , they would remember what God had done for them. He knew how easily it is for us to forget.

I would suggest you read Joshua 4:1-8 for the full story of the 12 stones of remembrance.

Exodus 14:14 The Lord shall fight for you, and ye shall hold your peace.

January 5

<u>Too blessed to be stressed</u>

Lord please help me to see that I need you just as much on the good days as I do on the bad.

It's easy to forget how much we depend on God when our day is going smoothly. Throw in a traffic jam, a few mishaps at work and all of sudden we are back to seeing how we need God every minute of every day.

What I have learned is that in the tough times is when I have walked closer to God. I see just how small I am. God shows up in those moments in a big way and suddenly all my problems feel smaller.

The Lord God is my strength, and he will make my feet like hinds' feet, and he will make me walk upon mine high places. To the chief singer on my stringed instruments. - Habakkuk 3:19

January 6

Refuge and Strength

There will always be times of trouble in this life. During the hard times God never leaves us. He assures us that He will get us through it.

It is all about your perspective. If you are looking for things to be grateful for and happy about, that is what you will see. If you are always looking for things that are wrong, and focusing on every negative thing that happens, that is what you will see.

It's kind of like when you buy a new white car and suddenly notice just how many white cars are on the road. It is because you are now looking for white cars.

Change what you are looking for and it will change everything! Look for the good, the positive, the reasons to be happy and that is what you will find!

"God is our refuge and strength a very present help in trouble"- Psalm 46:1

"And be not conformed to this world: but be ye transformed by the renewing of your mind that ye may prove what is that good, and acceptable and perfect, will of God".- Romans 12:2

January 7

Eyes to see and ears to hear

I pray often to have eyes that truly see and ears that hear. Sometimes I think we miss a lot. Not intentionally. Sometimes we are too close to the issue. Other times, I think our own personal issues get in the way. This clouds our vision and stops us from hearing. I think when we pray for understanding we have to be prepared to truly listen and see those around us and their needs. If we truly want to be the hands and feet of Jesus we have to be concerned about the things that He is concerned about. God loves people. He loves all people even with their messes and their issues.

"For the Son of man is come to seek and save that which is lost"- Luke 19: 10

"For God so loved the world, that he gave his only begotten Son, that whosoever believeth in him should not perish, but have everlasting life."- John 3:16

"But God commendeth his love toward us, in that, while we were yet sinners, Christ died for us. "- Romans 5:8

January 8

Assume the best

Sometimes we can be quick to judge others. I am as guilty as anyone of this. And often times I am wrong about what people's motives have been. I think sometimes we think the worst. We assume the worst with very little reasoning. I wonder why? I think it has a lot to do with our human nature. I think our sin nature leads us to think the worst. Our emotions can't be trusted. They change with our current feelings based on the situation at hand. I think it's said best that feelings aren't facts. God sent his son to die for us before we were even sorry, while we were still sinners. Can't we give others the benefit of the doubt?

"Therefore judge nothing before the time, until the Lord come, who both will bring to light the hidden things of darkness, and will make manifest the counsels of the hearts: and then shall every man have praise of God". -1 Corinthians 4:5

January 9

Faith

"And Jesus said unto them "Because of your unbelief: for verily I say unto you, If ye have faith as a grain of mustard seed, ye shall say unto this mountain, Remove hence to yonder place; and it shall remove; and nothing shall be impossible unto you" - Matthew 17-20-21

"And the Lord said, "If ye had faith as a grain of mustard seed, ye might say unto this sycamine tree, Be though plucked up by the root, and be thou planted in the sea; and it should obey you" - Luke 17:6

Ever seen a mustard seed? It's small. It seems insignificant. I think it proves just how powerful faith is. The tiniest amount can do mighty things.

I love how Jesus uses parables to help us understand. He says things in a way so they resonate with us. It makes them more memorable.

"Jesus said unto him If thou canst believe, all things are possible to him that believeth"- Mark 9:23

January 10

He reigns above it all

If you spend any time with me at all you have heard me say "God's ways are greater than our ways". Usually if you ask me a question and I really don't know why something happened, that is my standard response. It's true. Sometimes we will not understand why something happened the way it did. All I know is God can turn what was meant for evil into good. He knows all and is over all. I don't know the reasons but I do trust His plans.

"And we know that all things work together for good to them that love God, to them who are called according to his purpose"- Romans 8:28

"But as for you, ye thought evil against me; but God meant it unto good, bring to pass, as it is this day, to save much people alive".- Genesis 50:20

January 11

Study God's word

Have you ever experienced a part of scripture just seem to lift off the page at ya? Maybe you have read this scripture hundreds of times but today it has brand new meaning. This is how God speaks to us some days.

"So then faith cometh by hearing, and hearing by the word of God. But I say Have they not heard? Yes verily, their sound went into all the earth, and their words unto the ends of the world. "- Romans 10:17-18

January 12

Potter and Clay

Sometimes when creating pottery there are mistakes made. When this happens does the potter throw out the clay? No, of course he doesn't. It's still valuable. He just reshapes and reforms it.

In Jeremiah the Lord uses this as an analogy for Israel and it applies to us his people too.

Sometimes God has to reshape us and remold us to get us where we should be.

"O house of Israel can I not do with you as this potter has done? declares the Lord. Behold like the clay in the potters hand, so are you in my hand, O house of Israel"- Jeremiah 18:6 ESV/crossway

January 13

Weird tree

I was thinking about a tree we have in our backyard this morning. It's our weird tree. Every year in fall it holds onto it's leaves a little longer than all the others and every spring it blooms a little later. By doing this, it stands out. Not because it's doing anything super special but because of it's timing. Every year I keep thinking it will catch up. And every year it consistently holds out. We can all learn a thing or two from this tree. The first thing is just be originally you. Don't try to rush and keep up with someone else's time. Secondly, don't give up on things too soon because of others. Just be you, even if you are weird or different. Do you and you will definitely stand out. I love that tree a little more now.

"Before I formed thee in the belly I knew thee; and before thou camest forth out of the womb I sanctified thee, and I ordained thee a prophet unto the nations" Jeremiah 1:5

January 14

Let it go

God doesn't remember our sins. Why do you keep rehashing and beating yourself up for them? The moment that you trusted Jesus Christ as your Lord and Savior you were wrapped in Christ's righteousness. Clothes in white, covered with his love and his blood that He shed for us all.

"As far as the east is from the west, so far hath He removed our transgressions from us."- Psalm 103:12

*I think it is described to us this way so our finite minds can comprehend the ,gravity of them truly being removed.

"But God commendeth his love toward us in that, while we were yet sinners, Christ died for us. Much more then, being now justified by his blood, we shall be saved from wrath through him." -Romans 5:8-9

January 15

It is ok to not be ok

Today is a hard day for me. On this day in 2023 I lost my little dog Finley. I loved him and think of him often. I do myself a disservice when I pretend everything is ok, and I have it all together. God uses our weaknesses to make us strong in Him.

Our circumstances always change. But God stays the same.

"Jesus Christ is the same yesterday, today, and forever. "- Hebrews 13:8 NKJV

Behold God is mighty and does not despise any; he is mighty in strength of understanding."- Job 36:5

January 16

If the Lord willing

If you are southern, I guarantee you have heard people say (especially older folks) "If the Lord willing" before they say their plans. Turns out it isn't just a southern thing its Biblical!

James 4:15 says " For that ye ought to say " If the Lord will, we shall live, and do this, or that."

It actually goes on to say in James 4:16 "But now ye rejoice in your boastings: all such rejoicing is evil ".

James 4:17 says " Therefore to him that knoweth to do good, and doeth not, to him it is a sin".

Now us southerners do like to add a little extra in for good measure. I have heard this version numerous times in my life. "If the Lord willing and the creek don't rise". You have gotta love the south.

So if you hear me say "If the Lord will" before anything I might do- just know it's not just the southern girl in me. It is me trying to be closer to Jesus and do what is right.

January 17

Don't throw the baby out with the bathwater

Southerners use this phrase a lot. It means don't throw away something valuable with something invaluable. Kind of like an avoidable error. Don't toss a relationship away because of a misunderstanding. Don't give up on your dream because you had a setback.

"Sin is always avoidable"- James 1:13

"Suffer not thy mouth to cause thy flesh to sin; neither say thou before the angel, that if was an error: wherefore should God be angry at thy voice, and destroy the work of thy hands"?

January 18

Loved more than you can imagine

There is only one you! God's love is unconditional and infinite. He loves us with agape.

"But God commendeth his love toward us, in that, while we were yet sinners, Christ died for us"- Romans 5:8

January 19

Only one you-

God knew all about you before you were born. He knows all your weaknesses and your strengths. He knows that sometimes you talk too loud and he knows how it breaks your heart to see someone in pain. He knows EVERYTHING! And guess what, He loves you!

There is only one you on this entire planet.

"Let each person lead the life that the Lord has assigned to him, and to which God has called him. This is my rule in all the church."- 1 Corinthians 7:17 ESV

" For he will complete what he appoints for me, and many such things are in his mind." - Job 23:14

"He who has begun a good work in you will complete it until the day of Jesus Christ"- Philippians 1:6

January 20

<u>Fighting Battles</u>

Sometimes all God is waiting for is for you to let him take control and then He will fight your battles for you. I'm not sure why we try everything on our own before we decide to give our problems to God.

"The Lord shall fight for you, and ye shall hold your peace."-Exodus 14:14

"Oh you shall not fear them, for it is the Lord your God who fights for you."-Deuteronomy 3:22

"No in all these things we are more than conquerors through him who loved us."-Romans 8:37 ESV

Be still, Let the Lord fight for you!

January 21

Each day is a gift

A while back I started a gratitude journal. Every evening I would write 5 things that I was grateful for.

Some days -especially if they were rough days- it seemed hard to write 5 things until I started to think about how very blessed I am!

I have a roof over my head, food, warm bed, great job, awesome family, great friends. When you stop to think about all the blessings 5 things are a breeze and sometimes just knowing that regardless of how my day went I was blessed beyond measure.

It makes you look at the day's events differently.

When you adapt an attitude of gratitude it changes your whole outlook on life. It makes you appreciate and be grateful for your blessings.

Each day is a precious gift from God.

January 22

Blessed beyond measure

Ever been around someone who was just blessed? They carry themselves differently. Ever wonder why that is? I would suggest they are walking in the blessings of God. God intended that for all of us. When we walk close to God we will experience things in our life and favor that wont come any other way.

"Draw nigh to God, and He will draw nigh to you. Cleanse your hands, ye sinners; and purify your hearts, ye double minded."- James 4:8

"And God is able to make all grace abound toward you, that ye, always having all sufficiency in all things may abound to every good work"- 2 Corinthians 9:8

"Blessed is the man that trusteth in the Lord, and whose hope the Lord is. For he shall be as a tree planted by the waters, and that spreadeth out her roots by the river, and shall not see when hest cometh, but her leaf shall be green; and shall not be careful in the year of drought, neither shall cease from yielding fruit."- Jeremiah 17:7-8

January 23

You are not alone

"And, behold, I am with thee, and will keep thee in all places whither thou goest, and will bring thee again into this land; for I will not leave thee, until I have done that which I have spoken to the of. "- Genesis 28:15

"I will instruct thee and teach thee in the way which though shalt go: I will guide thee with mine eye"- Psalm 32:8

"God has said, "Never will I leave you; never will I forsake you." So we say with confidence. "The Lord is my helper; I will not be afraid."- Hebrews 13:5-6

January 24

Good Shepherd

When was the last time you allowed yourself to lie down in green pastures?

Have you let go of all your worries, all your cares and just let Him, your shepherd, just watch over you? Let Him be concerned for dangers- just truly rested in His presence and know that He has got you?

"The Lord is my shepherd. I shall not want. He maketh me to lie down in green pastures: he leadeth me beside the still waters."-Psalm 23: 1-2 KJV

January 25

God's Friendship

"God friendship is for God worshippers. They are the ones he confides in. If I keep my eyes on God I won't trip over my own feet"- Psalm 25: 14-15 MSG

"Blessed is the people that know the joyful sound: they shall walk , O Lord, in the light of thy countenance. In thy name shall they rejoice all the day: and in thy righteousness shall they be exalted."-Psalm 89:15-16

January 26

A Picture is worth a thousand feelings

Have you ever had a smell take you back to a memory?

Have you ever heard a song and been transported back to a day from your past?

Pictures can also do that for me. A picture can immediately take me back to the feelings from the day photographed. I love photos. It captures memories and feelings for me.

"But Mary treasured up all these things, pondering them in her heart."- Luke 2:19 ESV

January 27

Trust and Wait

"So the Lord blessed the latter end of Job more than his beginning."- Job 42:12

Sometimes God puts desires in our heart. We need to stay close to God by prayer and by daily Bible study.

Sometimes what God asks us to do is not necessarily something we wanted to do, but if God brings you to it he will get you through it.

"Delight yourself in the Lord and he will give you the desires of your heart."- Psalm 37:4

"For I know the plans I have for you", declares the Lord, "plans to prosper you and not to harm you, plans to give you hope and a future"- Jeremiah 29:11 ESV

January 28

Guilt

Today is a hard day for me. January 28, 2022 my Father passed away. It was suddenly and unexpected. Sometimes I carry guilt wishing and thinking that I could have done more. If only this; if only we would have done that. The same when my little dog passed-guilt. And anyone knows me knows that I did everything I could for my Dad and my Finley.

Why is it that we feel this guilt? Maybe we feel this way because we are human? Maybe I feel this because I am a fixer and I want to fix things? Truly, I believe it is Satan, the enemy. If he can't have you, then he wants to make your time less enjoyable here on Earth. He tries all he can.

I have learned that God's ways are not my ways. I don't understand the big picture. I miss my Dad every day. I wish we got more time together. But if he lived to be 100 years old I would still wish that! We never feel like it is enough. I will see him again though.

"And this is the will of him that sent me, that every one which seeth the Son, and believeth on him, may have everlasting life: and I will raise him up at the last day. "- John 6:40

January 29

Be happy

Be happy and do good. Don't let your happiness be determined by circumstances. It is all about perspective.

I hope the Lord shines on you today. I hope he covers you with so much love and happiness that your only option is to smile.

"The Lord make his face shine upon you, and be gracious to you. The Lord lift up his countenance upon you, and give you peace."- Numbers 6 :25-26 NKJV

"But godliness with contentment is great gain." 1 Timothy 6:6

"I know both how to be abased, and I know how to abound: everywhere and in all things I am instructed both to be full and to be hungry, both to abound and to suffer need."- Philippians 4:12

January 30

<u>Time</u>

There never seems to be enough time. But don't skimp on your time with Jesus. He can help you accomplish more in less time by spending quality time with him. Time in His presence changes your whole attitude and outlook.

"For through wisdom your days will be many, and years will be added to your life."- Proverbs 9:11 NIV

Whatever we give to God He will bless and multiply back to us, whether time or money.

"Give and it will be given to you. A good measure, pressed down, shaken together and running over, will be poured into your lap. For with the measure you use, it will be measured to you."- Luke 6:38

" I wait for the Lord, my soul doth wait, and in His word I do hope. My soul waiteth for the Lord more than they that watch for the morning: I say, more than they that watch for the morning."- Psalm 130:5-6

January 31

<u>Be your own sunshine</u>

If you can't find the sunshine, be the sunshine.

Happiness and smiles are free. Share it everywhere you go, all over, with everyone. The best part is that it is contagious!

Look for the good in your life and you will surely find it.

"May the Lord bless you and protect you. May the Lord smile on you and be gracious to you. May the Lord show you his favor and give you His peace"- Numbers 6:24-26

February 1

God's love

I was pondering on the love of God. If you have children you know as a parent that you will do anything to protect them. You would do anything to keep them safe from harm. As a matter of fact, you would do anything in your power to take away their pain even taking it upon yourself. We are merely human, flawed by birth.

Imagine someone asking you to sacrifice your child, for the worst person alive, maybe a murderer, a thief or a terrorist. What would your response be? Then think about God. All knowing, all loving, source of light, sending his Son to this earth because He loved us (sinners, murderers, liars, thieves, cheats, haters) so much that He couldn't bear for us to have no way to rectify our sins. Because, He knows that we could never be good enough on our own. So, He sent his only Son, spotless, blameless, without any sin, to be that sacrifice for all of us while we were yet sinners. That is how much God loves you!

"For God so loved the world, that he gave his only begotten Son, that whosoever believeth in him should not perish, but have everlasting life."- John 3:16

February 2

<u>Gratefulness</u>

There are so many things to be thankful for. Years ago, I started a gratitude journal. My goal was everyday to write (at least) 5 things that I was grateful for. On good days it was easy, and on rough days not so easy until I started looking at my list from the days before. Those things that I felt grateful for on previous days, were still in my life. I was still grateful for them. What changed? My attitude and my perception of my situation was the only thing that had changed. Sometimes we let small hurdles become mountains. Don't let things that won't matter tomorrow steal your joy today!

"Be glad in the Lord, and rejoice, ye righteous: and shout for joy, all ye that are upright in heart."- Psalm 32:11

"Let your moderation be known unto all men. The Lord is at hand. Be careful for nothing; but in everything by prayer and supplication with thanksgiving let your requests be made known unto God. "- Philippians 4:4

February 3

<u>Prayer</u>

Prayer is powerful. I would encourage you to start a prayer journal. In this journal you can list those who you want to pray for and what you are praying for. I also like to write my prayers out. It is amazing when you look back on what you were praying for and you can see how those things came to pass.

Curious how your life is going and what is important to you? Look back at your prayer journal.

Prayer changes things!

"Let your moderation be known unto all men. The Lord is at hand. Be careful for nothing; but in everything by prayer and supplication with thanksgiving let your requests be made known unto God. "-Philippians 4:4

February 4

How Wonderful God is

Let's be about God's work telling others how wonderful God is. He can turn trouble into triumph. He never leaves us!

Sometimes as Christians, I think we get too focused on small mishaps and forget others are watching us. My God is good and He does good. He loves me unconditionally. Let's not do God a disservice by focusing on the small things. Let's remember that we are redeemed, covered in his righteousness. We have a home in heaven, never to die. There will be no more tears in heaven. Let's live today being thankful for what we know our future holds. Let's show others just how wonderful our God is!

"The Lord they God in the midst of thee is mighty; he will save, he will rejoice over thee with joy; he will rest in his love, he will joy over thee with singing."-Zephaniah 3:17

Praise ye the Lord, Praise God in his sanctuary: praise him in the firmament of his power. Praise him for his mighty acts: praise him according to his excellent greatness. Let everything that hath breath praise the Lord. Praise ye the Lord-Psalm 150: 1-2, 6

February 5

Unrecognized Blessings

I was thinking today as I was cleaning out my car and ran across a penny- I wonder how many people have held the 1943D Bronze Lincoln penny in their hands and not realized just what they had. Last I looked it is valued at $1,700,000. Sometimes I think we get so used to things we miss the big blessings in our life- Something so simple as checking the change in your pocket could change your life.

What about that baby boy or girl in your arms?

What is their value?

Priceless-

Don't become so used to your everyday life that you forget exactly how blessed you are. Look for the value in everything around you.

"Godliness with contentment is great gain"- I Timothy 6:6

February 6

Unequally yoked

I was doing some reading and learned that 2 animals of different sizes and strengths shouldn't be yoked together because the smaller, weaker animal would be in constant pain and pressure.

Which got me to thinking- Jesus is stronger than I am but He promises that if we are yoked with him that the burden will be light. I think it is saying that when we trust him fully that we are clothed in his righteousness and therefore he takes on all the heavy lifting.

We have all likely heard the scripture: "Come unto me, all ye that labour and are heavy laden, and I will give you rest. Take my yoke upon you, and learn of me; for I am meek and lowly in heart: and ye shall find rest unto your souls."- Matthew 11:28-29

"Be ye not unequally yoked together with unbelievers: for what fellowship hath righteousness with unrighteousness? And what communion hath light with darkness "- 2 Corinthians 6:14

February 7

Protected

Everyone likes to feel safe and protected. I remember when I was pregnant with my first child, Makayla. My husband and I went to a church event. It was at the Grand Palace Theater in Branson, MO. Our seats were pretty high up and I was pretty expectant and had a pretty large belly at the time.

I have never forgotten how protected I felt. Everyone that we encountered was so helpful and it seemed that they had my best interest at heart. There is just something about that feeling. Almost like a shield, a barrier from all harm. That is what our God is for us. He is a protector, a shield and a barrier.

But you, Lord are a shield around me; my glory, and the lifter up of mine head."- Psalm 3:3

February 8

Awake

Have you ever thought that when you are awakened in the middle of the night, that it is because God wants to talk to you? Or maybe God wants you to talk to Him. I encourage you to use this "awake" time to speak to your creator. In doing so, he will give you peace and all the rest you need.

"I will both lay me down in peace, and sleep: For thou, Lord, only makes me dwell in safety. "- Psalm 4:8

February 9

Aerial Views

God doesn't give us aerial views. We don't get to see the big picture- no God's eye view. He lets us know step by step in faith as we take them trusting him. That's how faith works. You can't see what's around the bend but you know who is guiding you.

"A man's heart deviseth his way: but the Lord directeth his steps. " - Proverbs 16:9

February 10

The shepherd

Are you listening for God's voice? Would you recognize it from all the other things fighting for your attention?

Make sure that you set aside time to be alone with God to learn how to better hear his voice.

"My sheep hear my voice, and I know them, and they follow me"
John 10:27

February 11

What are you seeking?

Do you have zeal for the things of God?

"For where your treasure is there your heart will be also."- Matthew 6:21

The word "seek" in Hebrew means to search out by any method.

"Delight yourself in the Lord, and he will give you the desires of your heart"- Psalm 37:4

February 12

Small Beginnings

Do not despise small beginnings. When Danny and I got married, almost everything in our small apartment was things that others had given to us. Everything from our bed to our couch even our papason chair were hand me downs. I loved that space immensely! It was the beginning of us and our life together. It didn't matter that it was mismatched or used. It was now "ours" together.

We have been married for many years now and purchased all kinds of furniture. But when I think back to those apartment days, there is nothing but thoughts of how happy we were.

February 13

Imperfect people

Remember God uses imperfect people to share his word. Guess what? That's all we as people are is imperfect.

You can strive to be better, and that is wonderful. I encourage you to do so. But none of us can ever be perfect. Only one was ever perfect, Jesus, and he came here to die for us.

You will always find flaws with any man.

February 14

Blessed

How thankful are you today? Regardless of your feelings and situations, are you happy? If we get stuck on the negative we over look the positive blessings poured out daily to us.

Think of it like this, when you buy a white car you start to notice more white cars. What you look for and pay more attention to is what we see.

"Give thanks in all circumstances, for this is God's will for you in Christ Jesus."- 1 Thessalonians 5:18

February 15

The Unseen

Have you ever walked outside at night and spotted a star? When you began to look closely at it, just like magic, you started to see more stars. And before long the whole sky was filled with stars that a few moments before you couldn't see!

Some things don't reveal themselves until we focus.

They were always there; we just couldn't see them.

I think this is the perfect way to describe life before Jesus. He has always been there- we just couldn't see him.

"For with thee is the fountain of life: in thy light shall we see light. "- Psalm 36:9

February 16

The First Step

Sometimes God tells us to do things not knowing what lies ahead. He wants you to take the first step in faith and He will guide you from that moment. Sometimes, the first step is the hardest but the first step in the right direction is the most powerful. Let God lead you today to take the first step. And He will meet you there.

"The steps of a good man are ordered by the Lord: and he delighteth in his way. Though he fall, he shall not be utterly cast down: for the Lord upholdeth him with his hand. "- Psalm 37: 23-24

February 17

It's ok to ask for help

God gives us friends so we don't have to go through this life alone. You need one. We hold each other up when we get weak.

The paralytic man's 4 friends in Mark 2:1-5 who brought him to Jesus is the ultimate friend goal.

Are your friends willing to get you to Jesus no matter what or how? We should all be so lucky to have friends like this.

These friends didn't care about conventional ways, they had to get their friend to Jesus. They knew if they could just get him to Jesus, even if it meant dropping him through the ceiling, they knew Jesus would heal him.

Matthew 9:1-8

Luke 5:17-26

"A man that hath friends must shew himself friendly: and there is a friend that sticketh closer than a brother."- Proverbs 18:24

February 18

Be good to you

If you spoke to your friends like you often speak to and about yourself, how many friends would you still have?

Remember your body belongs to God.

He is a marvelous and wonderful creator.

He makes no mistakes.

You are human and that means that you are not perfect. Our goal is to keep striving to be like Jesus. You will make mistakes and ideally you will learn from them. Use these as opportunities to draw closer to God. I am glad that He does not require perfection.

"Because of the Lord's great love we are not consumed, for his compassions never fail"- Lamentations 3:22

February 19

<u>Blank Canvas</u>

God can do more for you and through you when you have a grateful and thankful heart. Think of it like an artist would a blank canvas, so many possibilities. There are no limits to what you can create with a blank canvas. Be transformable.

" And be not conformed to this world: but be ye transformed by the renewing of your mind, that ye may prove what is that good, and acceptable, and perfect will of God"- Romans 12:2

February 20

<u>Vulnerable</u>

Are you vulnerable to God?

Is He truly in charge?

Is He driving?

Only when you truly trust Him can He lead you where you need to be. What is it about the word vulnerable that strikes fear into the hearts of many? I think because when you are vulnerable to the things of the world it is a negative thing. You are exposed, maybe even endangered or liable. But when you are vulnerable to the things of God you are sensitive to His presence, open to His communication and subject to His plans for you. Being vulnerable to God makes you stronger not weaker, more powerful, not helpless.

"Humble yourselves in the sight of the Lord and He shall lift you up. "- James 4:10

February 21

Don't put God in a box

Are you limiting what God can do? Sometimes I think people are more comfortable to only expect small things from God. It scares them to think about God doing the impossible. God can do anything. God is God. Some things our human minds can't comprehend the how but we can still know it happened. Be hungry for all God wants to do, even the parts that take you out of your comfort zone. Outside of your comfort zone is when you start to understand and see just how mighty, large and great our God truly is.

"Now to him who is able to do immeasurably more than we ask or imagine according to his power that is at work within us"- Ephesians 3:20

February 22

Be expectant

Have you ever just been so excited for something? You couldn't wait to see what happened. Maybe it was a concert. Maybe watching a television series, maybe it was an upcoming birthday. It was just the surprise of the unknown. Why don't we approach God the same way? So excited to see what He has in store for us.

Pray for and expect more of His spirit. See how he works things out for your good. See how He goes before you in situations and opens doors. Expect and receive! You have not because you ask not.

"In the morning, O Lord, you hear my voice; in the morning I lay my requests before you and wait with expectation"- Psalm 5:3

"Ye lust, and have not: ye kill, and desire to have, and cannot obtain: ye fight and war, yet ye have not, because ye ask not."- James 4:2

February 23

Lack of faith and understanding

Sometimes we need to get away to a quiet place. Even Jesus did at least twice in the scriptures.

The disciples walked side by side with Jesus and saw him do many miracles, yet they still had little faith at times.

The questions and statements Jesus says should still apply to us today.

He asks them:

"Are you also still without understanding?"

"Do you not see?"

"O you of little faith why did you doubt?"

Matthew 14 and Matthew 15

February 24

Trust and Believe

What and how much does it take for us to truly trust and believe? If your story of all God has done for you was written down, would those reading it feel like we feel when we read about the disciples? Of all they have seen and experienced, all the miracles and still they doubt.

Seems unheard of right?

Trust and believe.

Start a journal of all that God has done for you and in times of doubt look back and see all that he has brought you through.

February 25

A quiet place

Time alone is necessary. So much can happen when you set aside time to be alone in God's presence. Even if you are running low on time, don't skimp with your time with Him. He can help you do more with less time after alone time with Him. It is worth it.

God knows it all, our heartache- our aches and pains of this world- He sees us when we are happy and sad and loves us just the same- today, tomorrow and forever.

"Lead me in Your truth and teach me, for You are the God of my salvation; for You I wait all day long. "- Palm 25:5

February 26

Happiness

Some things that bring me joy is hearing my daughter practicing her saxophone, waking up to hear the birds chirping as I have my coffee. There are so many other things that bring me happiness and joy. We need to appreciate the small things, as many times they are anything but small.

Make a list of all the things that bring you happiness. Then try to make sure that you are doing more of those things.

Life is too short to not be happy.

February 27

Many Names of God

God has many names. They all mean so many different things. But He is one in the same. He is the Lord God almighty, our healer, our provider and our protector.

Yahweh- Lord, Jehovah

Jehovah Rapha- The Lord that heals

Jehovah Jireh- The Lord our Provider

El Shaddai- Lord God Almighty

Elohim- God

Elohim Shomri- God is my protector

"I am the Lord thy God, which have brought thee out of the land of Egypt, out of the house of bondage. "- Exodus 20:2

February 28

Let go

I am so guilty of trying to preplan everything. With some things its helpful but with others it is a hindrance. There is just something about that sense of control, even if it is a false sense. We need to understand that God is still in control, and that is ok!

I don't have to hold on to the reins so tight. He's got me (and you too).

"Be still, and know that I am God: I will be exalted among the heathen, I will be exalted in the earth. "- Psalm 46:10

February 29

Peace

That word means so many things to so many people.

For some people it is a feeling.

For some it is freedom.

For me it is both but I love that my peace is not based on circumstances or situations. Matter of fact it isn't even just feelings, my peace is deep rooted inside me.

"And the peace of God, which passeth all understanding, shall keep your hearts and minds through Christ Jesus"- Philippians 4:7

"If the son therefore shall make you free, ye shall be free indeed."-
John 8:36

March 1

The motions

Are you just going through the motions in your prayer life?

Are you checking off a certain set of boxes?

Or are you earnestly asking and expectantly waiting? Does it help to know there is not a need he can't meet? Are you praying for those around you? If the only prayers prayed for your family and friends are yours, are they enough? Cover those you know and love (and even some you don't) in prayer.

"Praying always with all prayer and supplication in the Spirit, and watching thereunto with all perseverance and supplication for all saints;"- Ephesians 6:18

Keep your prayer journal full of needs and you will always have plenty to thank Him for.

Don't forget to praise Him in advance.

March 2

Ray of light in a sea of darkness

Your mission today, is to be a blessing to others.

Sometimes a simple smile or an act of kindness can make all the difference in someone's life.

Seek these people and these moments out. Help people to see Jesus' love pouring from you. For some people your life is the only church service they will attend. How can you show them Jesus?

"No man, when he hath lighted a candle, covereth it with a vessel, or putteth it in under a bed; but setteth it on a candlestick, that they which enter in may see the light"- Luke 8:16

March 3

Expiration dates

We always check them- it makes us feel better to see how long the milk will last or when to toss out the expired salad dressing- but have you ever thought that we have an expiration date too?

I have often heard nurses say "the patient expired" and recently I was just thinking about that.

None of us know exactly when our expiration date is. That is why we should live each day to the fullest and if your date is up know that you are ready to go. What is in store for the believer is better than life here.

"For me to live is Christ, and to die is gain"- Philippians 1:21

Also I suggest reading Philippians1:21-30

March 4

Thankful

What if the only things you were left with today were the things you thanked God for yesterday? How would you be? Have you thanked him for your family (spouse, kids, grandkids, and parents), your health, your marriage, your pets, your job, your house, your cars, your friends, your freedom, your church, your pastor, your bank account, your salvation?

You can't ever be too thankful or too grateful.

A thankful heart produces more things to be thankful for.

"O give thanks unto the Lord; for he is good; for his mercy endureth for ever. "- 1 Chronicles 16:34

March 5

Do-overs

Aren't there just some days you would like a do- over?

Wouldn't you like the chance to do some things differently?

Well as far as I know there is no time machine. You cant go back and re-do but you can make changes going forward.

Make sure that you don't beat yourself up too much over mistakes. We all make them. Hey we aren't perfect only one ever was. I know that when you are feeling the effects from a mistake made it can seem like all that there is but like your elders always used to tell ya "this too shall pass".

"Trust in the Lord with all your heart, and do not lean on your understanding. In all your ways acknowledge him, and he will make straight your path" -

Proverbs 3:5-6

March 6

<u>New Day</u>

Every breath is a gift-

Let God use your shortcomings to his advantage.

Circumstances don't determine your happiness.

Be steadfast in doing what is right, even if you seem to be the only one doing it.

"I can do all things through Christ, who strengthens me."- Philippians 4:13 NKJV

March 7

<u>Individual</u>

Individual, personal. He meets us where we are.

God has individual relationships with us all. What works for me may not work for someone else. I am individual and unique (it's how he created me!)

Jesus is a personal Savior!

He created us all with unique talents and gifts. There are things that only we can do for Him.

Never forget how special you are to Him!

Psalm 139:13-14

Psalm 33: 14-15 NKJV

March 8

Mindset

How many of us have something happen and we get all in our "feels" and let it define our day? I do. Matter of fact I did this just yesterday. I got a big project at work (a couple actually) -no problem. I love to be busy. Then one thing after another happens and BOOM! I'm in my own little pity party. Shame on me!

Instead of focusing on the current set of circumstances or problems, stop and see the big picture.

I am a child of GOD. I am loved by the most High.

I decide how I react to issues.

I have been forgiven of it all. It is well with my soul.

Don't let silly circumstances or a tainted mindset rob you of your joy. Every day is precious.

We all have loved ones not here with us. If we won't do it for ourselves, let's do it for them. LIVE, joyously and to the fullest.

"May the Lord of peace Himself give you peace at all times and in every way."- 2 Thessalonians 3:16

March 9

Control your mind

Satan tries to use anything he can. Sometimes he can use our own minds against us.

Say you enjoyed that Sunday morning service. Throughout the day Satan tries to pick it a part. Those songs were too long. They played the music too loud. The baby in the front was distracting. Satan will use anything to take away the actual message that you received.

He will use you to do the same when you share these things with others. Don't let Satan rob you of the blessings and encouragement that God gives you and certainly don't be the reason he robs others. If you can't say something nice and helpful, it's probably best to stay silent.

Create in me a clean heart, O God, and renew a steadfast spirit within me. - Psalm 51:10

March 10

Tempted

As I was reading Luke 4: 1-13 this morning, I noticed how persistent the devil is at tempting Jesus.

The devil didn't try once and gave up. He tried numerous times. He offered things he thought Jesus would want. He tempted Jesus using scripture, but incorrectly. And finally it says in the ESV version Luke 4:13 "And when the devil had ended every temptation, he departed from him until an opportune time."

In reading this, I realized the devil had tempted him every day but he waited until Jesus had been fasting for 40 days and was hungry and then he came to him asking him to turn the rocks to bread. He was waiting for that opportune time. The devil works this way with us to this day. He usually waits until you are at your weakest, almost to the breaking point and then taunts you and then shows up as everything you wanted, immediate gratification, sneaky, manipulative, cunning, trying to get you to doubt how big your GOD is! If he was persistent with Jesus, why do you think we are any different? We can't let him get a foothold!

I like how the bible tells us that Jesus was hungry. It gives us a glimpse of the humanness, I think so we can relate.

Remember Satan is a liar and the father of Lies- John 8:44

Jesus used God's word as his response. I love how by quoting God's word Jesus shows us just how powerful it is in defeating Satan.

"Be sober, be vigilant; because your adversary the devil, as a roaring lion, walketh about, seeking whom he my devour."- 1 Peter 5:8

March 11

Busy

Anyone else super busy these days?

Seems we all have so many things asking for our attention.

Make sure that you make time and take time to talk to God. It makes everything so much better. You don't have to plan everything. Sometimes no maps are needed. (I know it is a work in progress for me too) But make sure to plan "empty days", days with absolutely nothing on the agenda. Those are important too.

Even God knew rest was important.

If he rested shouldn't you?

Genesis 2:2-3

March 12

Covered

What if today you could see yourself as God sees you? Clothed in the righteousness of Jesus, enough, loved, beautiful, exactly how and where you are supposed to be.

"Commit your work to the Lord and your plans will be established" -Proverbs 16:3 ESV

"The lord has made everything for its purpose even the wicked for the day of trouble" -Proverbs 16:4 ESV

"When a man's ways please the Lord he makes even his enemies be at peace with him"- Proverbs 16:7 ESV

"The heart of man plans his way but the Lord establishes his steps" - Proverbs 16:9 ESV

March 13

Only God

Remember this: God doesn't love you because of anything that you can do or have done. He simply loves you because He is God. It is who God is.

Being grateful for all God is, is the beginning to happiness. When you realize it's not about you, it takes a lot of worry and weight off of your shoulders. None of us can ever be or do enough to earn God's love. Thank God because of Jesus we are enough. He did what no human could ever do. Simply because He loves you!

"For God so loved the world that he gave his only begotten Son, that whosoever believeth in him should not perish, but have everlasting life." - John 3:16

"No eye has seen, no ear has heard, and no mind has imagined what God has prepared for those who love Him"- 1 Corinthians 2:9

Read: Ephesians 3:18-19

March 14

God's Plans

God has great plans for each of us. We have to let go of the reins and let God direct us. He created you with potential for His purpose.

"The Lord gives wisdom from his mouth come knowledge and understanding" - Proverbs 2:6

Pray about your decisions for your future. Let God lead you.

Read 2 Timothy 2:13 NIV

March 15

Choose your words

Words are powerful. They have the power to build up or tear down. What are you speaking into people's lives?

I have heard this all my life- before you say something ask yourself; Is it true? Is it kind? Is it necessary? If the answer is no to any of these, it is probably best not to say it.

The Bible talks about how powerful words are and how destructive the tongue can be.

" DO not let any unwholesome talk come out of your mouths, but only what is helpful for building others according to their needs; that it may benefit those that listen" Ephesians 4:29

Read James 3:3-6

The book of Proverbs also has a lot of encouraging words.

March 16

Sluggish

Ever have those days where you just want to stay home? Ever have moments where you do not want to have any responsibilities? Yes, me too! But remember, each day is a gift. Many others don't get the chance to be here today.

Shake off that negativity and shine.

Someone is counting on your smile today.

"This is the day which the Lord hath made ; we will rejoice and be glad in it"- Psalm 118:24

March 17

Seeing is not believing

Ever watched something in such amazement to only realize it was fake?

I remember a video many years ago of a dog putting on Sunglasses. Oh my gosh, how impressed I was with that dog, until my kids told me it was played in reverse. The dog was actually removing the glasses. How let down I was and disappointed. Sometimes we get all caught up in what we see. Especially if things are going all wrong or maybe not at all the way you hoped.

There is so much that is unseen. Some of the truest things in this world aren't seen. Love, air, the spiritual realm are just a few. Don't get caught up on just what you can see today. Set your sights on something bigger.

"We walk by faith-not by sight" 2 Corinthians 5:7 NKJV

March 18

God calls us all

Is God calling you to a higher place? Don't be afraid- step into what He has for you. God equips us with what we need to finish his work that he has for us. Let him take you higher.

Philippians 1:6 says" Being confident of this very thing, that he which hath begun a good work in you will perform it until the day of Jesus Christ."

March 19

Look to Jesus

There will always be problems in this world.

If you make sure your focus is on Jesus you will have less time to focus on your problems.

We were created to look at and to God for your source of help.

"In everything give thanks: for this is the will of God in Christ Jesus concerning you"- 1 Thessalonians 5:18

"My help cometh from the Lord, which made heaven and earth"- Psalm 121:2

March 20

Satan

Satan tries to accuse us. He is happiest when he is heaping feelings of guilt upon us. As believers, he wants us covered with feelings of guilt. It's easier to shame us. All of this is intended to keep you from having joy. It is all to encourage you to doubt God and His wisdom. We won't understand a lot of things that happen in this world. And that is ok as long as we remember that God is good and He does good. The devil is a liar.

Remember Satan is a liar and the father of Lies- John 8:44

"Be sober, be vigilant; because your adversary the devil, as a roaring lion, walketh about, seeking whom he my devour."- 1 Peter 5:8

March 21

The struggle is real

I watched a video this morning where a drummer had a fake tree falling on him while he was trying to play a worship song. It was a really good look into how Satan works. The drummer was doing his best to try to fight the tree off with one hand and still play the worship song with his other. Isn't that just the way it feels sometimes? We have things trying to distract us from the things of God. In the video the singer never noticed all this and just kept right on worshipping. This also made me think; people can be close to us and never see what we are fighting. My friend Shannon even pointed out to me that the tree is fake- not real or it would be standing tall for the creator. There is a lot to ponder here. Not everything is at it seems.

Read Philippians 4:8

Isaiah 26:3-4

March 22

Harvest

My father was a great gardener. He enjoyed it. He knew that you planted with the harvest in mind. You sow seeds in the hopes that they grow and multiply your return.

What are you sowing in your life? Are you sowing seeds of goodness, honesty, love and kindness? The thing to remember is whatever you sow is what you reap. No one ever harvested blueberries if they planted kale.

Think more about the harvest. What do you want that to look like? Start planting seeds for that. And be patient. You don't get results right away. But the law of the harvest will prevail.

March 23

Bloom where you are planted

It is easy to get caught up in looking at other's lives and maybe even envying what they have going for them. With social media we have lots of opportunities to see all the cool and neat things others are doing and start to question our own lives. But don't compare yourself to anyone. You just be the best you that you can be. Think about flowers. They are so beautiful! But they are all very different. They have different leaves, different pedals, different colors and different smells. Because of how very different they are flower gardens are more beautiful. We each are created special, with a mission and a purpose to fulfill. Your pedals and your leaves are exactly what is needed for your mission. So, bloom where you are planted!

"We know that God causes everything to work together for the good of those who love God and are called according to His purpose for them."- Romans 8:28

March 24

Creature of Habit

Is anyone else a creature of habit? Do you follow the same route to work every day, eat the same foods, wake up and have the same routine?

If so, I think that it is important that people like us have to make sure that we are not just going through the motions in our lives. We need to be especially careful when it comes to our devotional time. Make sure you are not just checking off a box.

Don't be so caught up in your habits that you miss what God has for you. Stop, be present in each moment. In every menial task of your day see the beauty and wonder. We were created for more than just to exist.

God has great things for you; make sure that you are able to see them.

March 25

Your part

Are you doing your part to "draw others out of the darkness"? Why is it so hard for us to share about God's love with others? If Chic-fil-a were giving away free food, we would tell EVERYONE; because, we don't want them to miss out right? Well it's the same with God's love! I know some days it is the only thing holding me together. Share your faith with those close to you. Your love for God shouldn't be a secret.

Let's not keep something so valuable away from our loved ones.

"May you experience the love of Christ, though it is too great to understand fully. Then you will be made complete with all the fullness of life and power that comes from God."- Ephesians 3:19 NLT

"Happy are those who hear the joyful call to worship, for they will walk in the light of your Presence, Lord. They exult in your righteousness."- Psalm 89:15-16

March 26

Me time

Too much work makes you burn out quick. You must give yourself time to rest and unwind.

Spend time in your garden, take a walk, read a book or just be in your home.

Also, make sure you set aside your quiet time with God separately from your "me- time"

"God time" works on your heart and your soul and "me-time" works on your body and your mind. Both are important to your happiness.

"God is able to provide you with every blessing in abundance, so that having all sufficiency in all things at all times, you may abound in every good work." 2 Corinthians 9:8

March 27

Work for the Lord

A work friend & I were talking about how much we love our jobs. I feel blessed daily that I get to go to my job. Even when I have had not so good jobs, I have always showed up and gave it 100%. Why? I'm not working for my earthly boss but my Heavenly Father. I know I am where I belong and until further notice, it is where I will remain.

"And whatsoever ye do, do it heartily as to the Lord and not unto men"- Colossians 3:23 KJV

March 28

We are all even

As I was driving past a ceremony the other day I was thinking. Out there you cant tell who was wealthy. You can't tell from a cemetery who had a wonderful job or a large home. You can't tell out there who was a good person or who was a thief. You can't tell how many followers a person had or how popular they were on social media. From that final resting place, you can't tell much of anything; which led me to believe that it is perfect, because truly none of those things matter. So if at the end of your life those things aren't what is important; why stress so much over them now? At this point only one thing matters- Did you have a relationship with Jesus? Were you prepared to leave this world?

I have told my children that I want a headstone that is painted bright yellow and be like the sun!

March 29

Shepherd

The shepherd leaving the 99 to find the one doesn't mean much until you are the one he is coming to save.

I am so thankful for God's love and mercy!

"Cast all your anxiety on Him because He cares for you"- 1 Peter 5:7

March 30

Small stuff

Why is it we only get excited about the big stuff? Daily God gives us glorious sun rises and sunsets. We enjoy the warm sun or even sometimes the cool rain. We enjoy a light breeze on a warm day. We are serenaded by birds or crickets. I could go on and on. Do you sense God in these small moments? He is there. Just ask Him to give you eyes to see and ears to hear.

Don't live your life waiting for the next big thing. Enjoy the millions of small reasons to be happy. They are there, trust me, you just have to see them.

"Blessing and glory and wisdom and thanksgiving and honor and power and might to be our God forever and ever! Amen. "- Revelation 7:12

March 31

Only time

Don't let time be your downfall. God is timeless. Sometimes we like to think we have it all under control. We set aside time for this and time for that but don't rush through your time in God's presence. This time is too precious. It charges you, and gets you ready for anything that might come your way. Make sure there are no distractions so your focus can be only on God and his presence.

"We wait in hope for the Lord, he is our help and our shield"- Psalm 33:20

April 1

Unpack

We all carry around stuff with us; Hurts, past disappointments, worry. We drag around a lot of things we just need to lay down. Leave them behind. They do you no good. Fear, regret and hard feelings we need to give them up too. It's OK to travel light. CS Lewis said"It's not the load that ways you down, it's the way you carry it"

Some things you need to give to God and release them. Get some rest.

You will pick up many more "souvenirs" along the way. Don't carry more than you can handle- Share the load!

"Take my yoke upon you, and learn of me; for I am meek and lowly in heart: and ye shall find rest unto your souls. For my yoke is easy, and my burden is light. "- Matthew 11:29-30

April 2

<u>Kindness</u>

Don't wait until people are gone to try to show and tell them how much they mean to you.

Give people their flowers now.

No one is promised a tomorrow.

Sometimes a text or a kind word can make all the difference in someone's life. In some cases it could be the difference between life and death. Leave those that you interact with better than you found them.

Uplift and encourage people!

April 3

<u>Alone time</u>

Time; Have you mastered it or is it mastering you? There is a time for everything. Make sure you set aside "alone time". Set aside time for just you and God. Make sure to eliminate distractions. Make sure that you are not working on your to do lists for the day; Just you and God. Time spent with God makes the rest of your Day so much better.

"I am the living bread that came down from heaven. If anyone eats of this bread, he will live forever. "- John 6:51

April 4

<u>Not about you</u>

It is not about what you can do, But what He can do through you. Listen and obey and there is no limit to what God can do.

You never know what is going on behind the scenes. A simple card or text from you can be an answered pray for someone in need.

Be willing and available for God to use you.

April 5

<u>Same God</u>

God never changes. He is the same today, tomorrow and forever.

"For I am the Lord, I change not; therefore ye sons of Jacob are not consumed"- Malachi 3:6

"Every good gift and every perfect gift is from above and cometh down from the Father of lights with whom is no variableness, neither shadow of turning" - James 1:17

April 6

<u>Do over</u>

Ever do something and really wish you could get a "do over"? There are lots of things we wish we could take back whether its words said or things we have done. As far as I know there is no magic time machine that will let us go back and undo. But you can start today and do differently. Sometimes its apologizing for things said other times it is owning our mistakes and growing from them.

Sometimes it is just appreciating what we have more. Trust me I have done things that I so wanted to fix and some things can be fixed but others can never truly be the same. What I have learned from all my stressing and obsessing is that all the worry really did nothing but ruin my day and ruin my attitude; which kind of ruins the day of those around me.

If worry is drowning you, give it to God and let it go. Worry and stress fixes nothing. (Unless you like ulcers) Trust me. Putting it all out there and laying it down is the best for your soul (and your stomach).

April 7

Pot bound

Did you know that plants need to be repotted at least every 2 years so they don't get "pot-bound". You see all the nutrients in the soil gets used up and even if the plant doesn't need more room to grow it doesn't thrive anymore.

It happens to us too. Sometimes you need to loosen the soil around our souls, find something that sparks our imagination, quickens our pulse or just brings a smile to our faces. You have to get yourself into some nutrient rich soil!

Psalm 18:16-19 MSG

April 8

<u>Grace</u>

Thought for today, everyone has issues. Truly listen to that person that comes to you. Listen, not to respond, but listen to understand. When you truly understand what folks are going through it is much easier to extend grace.

"Forebearing one another, and forgoing one another, if any man have a quarrel against any: even as Christ forgave you, so also do ye" - Colossians 3:13

April 9

<u>Acronyms</u>

I'm glad that God created me a little different. I don't fall into the FOMO (fear of missing out) folks. Not all invitations need to be a yes. I'm getting better at saying no. I'm not a YOLO (you only live once) person either. I don't want an excuse to make frivolous decisions. I over think things sometimes. I know this life is not all there is. That affects some of my decisions. I want to get at better at being a BPITM (be present in the moment) person.

April 10

<u>Forgive me</u>

I sat and cried today watching a video of a child in another country so thankful to have clean water and to get a drink. We take so much for granted in this country. -Acts 10:43

April 11

Caffeine and weirdness

My day usually starts with coffee. My quiet time is spent at my kitchen table with my devotional; my bible and a cup of coffee. I like to spend my devotional time early in the morning while everyone else is sleeping. i am learning that everything doesn't have to be planned out. Most days if I have a plan it gets rewritten anyway. Make sure you aren't wasting all your time obsessing over plans. Sometimes you just need coffee, some trust, and faith. I always pack a little weirdness as well.

April 12

Clarity

Ever had days that you just have all kinds of clarity? You speak without reservation. You feel wonderful regardless of the day's events. I love those days. Then there are those days that I look for my phone while I'm talking on it. Balance- it's all about balance; just enough to not tip the scale.

I am thankful God lets me see; good and bad; happy and sad. It makes me understand and relate to people. We are all so very much alike.

April 13

Strength

During the hard times,(trials)of this life your faith is strengthened. God can use these circumstances to show you many things about yourself and about Him. He can show and prove to you His faithfulness. He can help you see that it is His strength not yours. -Psalms 46:1-3

April 14

Limiting God

Are you limiting God?

Don't put God in a box.

It is far more comfortable for people to limit what God can do.

I know that God can do anything.

I don't want to put limits on God because my human mind can't comprehend all that is possible.

April 15

Blend in

God designed you exactly how you are to bring honor and glory to him.

Don't try to blend in.

Be uniquely you.

April 16

<u>Prayer</u>

Prayer can change things.

Are you lifting those around you up?

Pray for your circle.

If Satan can't get to you, he will try to get to those closest to you.

April 17

<u>Never leaves</u>

Recently I realized that throughout my life Jesus was always with me; even when I knew nothing about Him.

I know that many times he kept me safe and helped me out of numerous situations; situations that I got myself into.

I look back now and think how blessed I am to be here. I know that God has a plan for my life.

April 18

<u>Relationships</u>

Relationships need to be nurtured. Pray for your spouse. Love is a daily decision and a commitment. God looks at the heart. How much better would our relationships be if we could see the heart?

God trusts us to be faithful in caring for our mate, our family, our friends and the calling he has put on our lives.

Obey God in all things.

April 19

Not alone

When problems come we are not alone. God cares for you more than you can imagine.

God loves you so much. He knows exactly how many hairs are on your head. I only have 3 children and I call them by the wrong names sometimes, but I love them beyond all words yet I have no idea how many hairs are on their heads; God knows!

Matthew 10:29-31

April 20

New Beginnings

Who else is terrified of new beginnings? They are scary, but they can also be filled with blessings.

I can't wait to see what and who God puts in my path next.

" For I know the plans I have for you declares the Lord plans to prosper you and not harm you plans to give you hope and a future"- Jeremiah 29:11

April 21

Laugh

Laugh at yourself more, be lighthearted and don't take yourself so seriously.

How will you be remembered?

What are you doing to make your life count?

"Happy is the man that findeth wisdom, and the man that getteth understanding."- Proverbs 3:13

April 22

Whitewash

God doesn't want our whitewashed selves. He wants the actual you. The parts of you that want to get even, parts that gossip, part that is frustrated with how things have turned out. He knows anyway. And he still loves you. He is waiting for you to bring it all to him; openly and honestly; even ugly crying. He is waiting to give you some answers. It may not be the answers that you want; it may put you on a better completely different path, but His ways are greater than our ways!

We need to focus on our hearts and let God focus on our plans.

"In their hearts humans plan their course, but the Lord establishes their steps"- Proverbs 16:9

April 23

Humble

"Do not think of yourself more highly than you ought"- Romans 12:3

April 24

Delays

Thank God for the delays.

What appears as a delay could be a redirection.

God's ways are so much greater than our ways.

Trust in His plan.

April 25

Hope

Sometimes the only thing to cling to is hope. Hope in a better day. Hope in a better situation. Hope in a different outcome. Hope in a better diagnosis. Always have hope, always share hope with others.

"Hope deferred makes the heart sick, but a dream fulfilled is a tree of life"- Proverbs 13:12

April 26

Unseen

Be more aware of unseen things as you live in this world. Some of the most real things in the world are not seen but felt!

"Faith is confidence in what we hope for and assurance about what we do not see"- Hebrews 11:1

April 27

Smile

I hope the Lord shines on you today. I hope he covers you with so much love and happiness your only option is to smile.

"The Lord makes His face shine upon you, and be gracious to you, The Lord lift up His countenance upon you and give you peace."- Numbers 6: 25-26

April 28

Time

We never have enough of it.

It's a very precious commodity.

We are born with a limited supply of it.

I think of an hour glass filled with sand. Most of us haven't mastered it yet.

We give it away so easily. Be more particular on where you spend most of your time. Unfortunately for some of us we have to work. So where some of our time goes is a necessity.

But for the free time how are you spending it?

Are you doing what makes you happy?

Spending it with those you love?

Make sure at the end of your time here on earth when your hour glass of time has almost run out that you have no regrets of how you chose to spend your precious time.

April 29

<u>Words</u>

Words can be like weapons or like medicine. Speak life into those around you. Leave them better than you found them.

Ask yourself, "Is it true, Is it kind, is it necessary?" If no is the answer to any of these questions then it is probably best not to say it.

Don't say things in anger that you'll regret. People may not remember everything that you say but they will remember how you made them feel.

"Wherefore my beloved Brothren, let every man be swift to hear, slow to speak and slow to wrath"- James 1 :19

April 30

<u>Companion</u>

God is with you every step of the walk.

 You are not alone.

I have always heard the saying that the teacher is always quiet during a test. I don't believe God tests us as much as encourages us and empowers us.

Sometimes our minds are too loud to hear him. We are the ones who need to quiet ourselves to hear him.

He usually speaks in a soft still voice.

1 Kings 19:11-13

May 1

Bless Others

God wired us to want to help others. We feel good when we can fulfill his purpose.

Sometimes work doesn't feel like work when you truly understand the good you are doing for His Kingdom.

"A Generous person will prosper; whoever refreshes others will be refreshed."- Proverbs 11:25

May 2

So much for granted

Lord please forgive me for all I take for granted. So many people who are struggling with diseases or with losing their homes to fire or devastation and I sit here in my air conditioned home with food in my fridge and coffee in my cup.

Pause- think about all you have to be thankful and grateful for.

Pray for those going through a rough season now.

May 3

Tell your story

Tell your story. How you made it through might be the only comfort someone has. Your story might be part of their roadmap for healing.

My book "Learning to live after loss" was published the year that I lost my Father.

My only goal is that it helps someone else who may be going through the worst season of their life.

"Your reward for trusting Him will be the salvation of your souls." - 1 Peter 1:9

May 4

Cruel World

The world might be harsh and cruel, but God is good. In Him there is no darkness.

God calls us to righteousness. Not ours but his. Which means to him you are good, moral, blameless, honest honorable and faithful.

God doesn't want you to live a guilt ridden life. He wants you to live a life covered by grace; His grace. He covered all our sin with His blood when He died on the cross for us.

"He who earnestly seeks good finds favor"- Proverbs 11:27

May 5

Bless the World

God will use you to bless others. Share all your blessings. God blesses us to be a blessing to others.

By the measure you give it will be given back to you.

And if you don't have anything to share, share a smile. They are free. They cost nothing but can change someone's day. And by changing someone's day you just might change their life!

Luke 6:38-40

May 6

<u>God's timing not mine</u>

Stop trying to "make" things happen. Do what God is requiring of you now and be patient.

All things will work together in His time.

Romans 8:28

May 7

<u>Instant Regret</u>

Anyone else have instant regret?

The moment you say something you shouldn't?

The moment you wish you would just have said no instead of yes.

So many things, sometimes quickly we know that oh my, one simple change in response could have had a very different outcome.

We don't get to redo things from our past but we can start from now and change how the future goes.

It's never too late for a new beginning.

Lamentations 3:22-23

Isaiah 43:19

May 8

Auto Pilot

Are you aware of your actions?

Are you present or just on auto pilot?

Make sure you are aware and are actually present not just going through the motions. Make conscious decisions on purpose.

Don't look back and realize that you missed out on a lot of things because you were on auto pilot.

May 9

Distracted

Do you often get distracted?

When you are distracted is it game over for you?

If so, remember that you have been given authority over all the distractions. Just focus. Get back to your duties. Do one thing at a time, one moment at a time. Walk steady, sure and focused on your tasks.

"Remain in me, and I will remain in you. No branch can bear fruit by itself; it must remain in the vine. Neither can you bear fruit unless you remain in me" - John 15:4

May 10

<u>Living for God</u>

You are never alone.

Nothing is too difficult for God.

Rejoice today in all that you have and all that you can be.

Rejoice today!

"But without faith it is impossible to please him: for he that cometh to God must believe that he is, and that he is a reward of them that diligently seek him."- Hebrews 11:6

May 11

<u>God sees</u>

God sees everything.

He knows everything.

He is so merciful and gracious that he wants none to perish but that all come to know him, but what do you think will be the final straw?

What will be the end?

When will he say- that's enough- I'm done?

I am so very glad that God's ways are greater than my ways . My patience level with the state of people and the world would not be very good measure. So very glad that God is good and does good.

Jeremiah 23:24

2 Peter 3:9

May 12

<u>Blessings</u>

Sometimes blessings come in the form of pain and trouble- as a friend at work said "The Lord is using this to teach you something"- what an exciting thing to think about. His ways are greater than my ways! What good will come from this?

Trust will keep you close to God let him calm your fears.

It is ok to not be okay. Better days are coming.

May 13

<u>Alone</u>

Even when you feel all alone, and wonder where God is; He is right there even closer than normal. God is at work in you to draw you closer to Him. Nothing can separate you from the love of God. Remember it is not about perfect circumstances. Even though you might not see it right now, God is working.

May 14

<u>Shortcomings</u>

God loves you regardless of your shortcomings.

 You cannot do enough good to earn God's love.

But I thank God that we don't have to.

God's love is unconditional.

May 15

<u>Humble</u>

Sometimes we are put in humbling situations so we can learn to be joyful anyway. It is about pushing through. God is still God no matter what the circumstances.

May 16

One day at a time

Live one day at a time.

There is a time and place for everything.

Be hopefully even in the most bleak circumstances.

Be strong.

"There is a time for every purpose and for every work"- Ecclesiastes 3:17

1 Corinthians 6:19-20

James 1:2-3

May 17

Laugh

Laugh at yourself more. Be happy. Don't take yourself too seriously.

How do you want to be remembered? What will you do to make your life count for Jesus?

God wants us to be faithful in what He has called you to do for him.

Romans 12:2

May 18

Rejoice

Rejoice in big and small things. Enjoy every moment of your life. There are no bad days. Look at your problems as blessings in disguise, see them as opportunities to get closer to God.

Decide to be happy.

Fix your thoughts on the good things and the positive things.

Be bold in your faith.

"Rejoice in the Lord always: and again I say, Rejoice"- Philippians 4:4

May 19

Map

God has your whole life mapped out.

Think about what you would do if you had no responsibilities, what would you still do for free, if money and time were no limit what would you do with your life?

I have heard that God's plan for you is somewhere in those questions. Think about what excites you, what you are passionate about and ask yourself why those things call to you. You may just find God has a purpose for you in using your passion.

"Take delight in the Lord and He will give you the desires of your heart"- Psalm 37:4

May 20

Eyes on God

Keep your eyes on God. If God is leading you to something he will equip you for the task at hand.

Always be thankful for your blessings. Make sure to take care of your body as it is a temple.

Quiet time with God is an important part of your selfcare.

May 21

Pray

Prayer is not as much about the words as long as you are sharing from your heart. God already knows.

Sometimes the best prayers are those that are barely understood by human ears.

Speak to your creator and pour out your heart.

He loves you.

May 22

<u>Joyful</u>

Attitude has a lot to do with how you operate in your daily life. Whatever you do, do it as if for the Lord.

You are fearfully and wonderfully made.

"The Lord has done great things for us, and we are filled with joy"- Psalm 126:3

1 Corinthians10:31

May 23

<u>Gift</u>

Each day is a gift.

Don't waste a single one!

You don't have to know every answer or what is happening next.

Relax.

Social media can be good as long as it is used to connect and encourage others. Don't get caught up with trying to outdo each other.

May 24

<u>Time</u>

Learn to master time or it will master you.

You are only given so many hours in a day. How are you spending yours?

Are you allowing a bad five minutes to dictate your whole day?

Keep in mind it is not what happens to you but how you react to what happens to you that matters.

May 25

<u>Facts aren't feelings</u>

These 2 things are totally independent. The enemy is a liar determined to tear us down and make us doubt ourselves, but most importantly he wants us to doubt God. If he can convince you to doubt what God said or all that God can do then he has you.

Try to look at yourself like God see's you; Covered in grace.

May 26

<u>Start small</u>

It's the little things that determine the big things.

Don't underestimate small beginnings. Just because you start small doesn't mean you can't finish big!

Let God's peace help you to eliminate fear in your daily life.

"Thou has been faithful over a few things, I will make thee ruler over many things: enter thou into the joy of the Lord" Matthew 25:21

May 27

Buckler

If you are going into this week tired, or this month has been the longest month ever or this year has been filled with so much loss or hurt and you are thinking you have no idea how you will ever make it through; Remember, God is our buckler. The bible uses the reference of God being a buckler several times.

"As for God, his way is perfect: the word of the Lord is tried: he is a buckler to all those that trust Him"- Psalm 18:30.

"He shall cover thee with his feathers, and under his wings shalt thou trust: His truth shall be thy shield and buckler."

Psalm 91:4 "He layeth up wisdom for the righteous: he is a buckler to them that walk uprightly."- Proverbs 2:7.

Now I had to google what a buckler was. A buckler is a "portable shield" also "a large shield protecting the whole body"- it refers to it as a defensive weapon used to ward off the attacks and blows of the enemy. So God is our shield, our protector!

May 28

Generous= happy

There are very few things that science and the word of God agree on, but our brains are wired to feel happier when we are generous. Generosity cultivates happiness. God created us that way and science proved it to be true. When we are generous our brain releases chemicals that give us a sense of joy and peace.

We never know how much a little kindness can mean to someone. What seems so trivial to you could mean everything to someone else.

"It is more blessed to give than to receive" Acts 20:35

May 29

Judgment

It is so easy to be judgmental. I think we all are guilty of this at times. And no one wants to feel like they are being judged. I get it. It stinks. If you start to see people like Jesus does, through his eyes it will change your perspective. It will be easier to show a little more grace.

"Judge not, that ye be not judged"- Mathew 7:1

May 30

Empty hands

Sometimes all we need is empty hands and an open heart. God doesn't need a lot of extras. He just needs you to give it all to him. He can do more with nothing than we can do with everything.

May 31

Rest

Even God set aside time for rest.

Why in the world would you think that it doesn't apply to you as well?

I have often heard if you don't pick a day to rest your body will pick one for you. You can't pour from an empty cup.

June 1

Talk to God

Make sure you talk to God before you talk to anyone else. It sets the tone for your day. That means with everything. God knows you better than anyone and still He loves you. Tell him your problems but also praise him for all your blessings. Remember part of having a conversation is listening as well. Pour your heart out but then listen. Hear what He has for you.

Philippians 4:6

June 2

Refuge

God is our refuge.

I googled refuge.

The definition is "being safe from danger or trouble".

How wonderful that is! God is providing us shelter from life's troubles.

Refresh others and be refreshed yourself.

"God is our refuge and strength, a very present help in trouble." - Psalm 46:1

June 3

<u>Rules</u>

Don't get caught up in the manmade rules of how to be a Christian.

We are to be little Christs.

Think about what Jesus would do.

Be more focused on God than on performance.

Worship the Lord with your whole heart.

Psalm 100:2

June 4

<u>Weakness</u>

God shows up in our weakness.

He uses what we see as weakness to appear strong.

God's power is perfected in our neediness and our weakness.

He uses us to make his ways known to the world.

Don't worry,if you are lacking God can use that.

June 5

Quietness

Sometimes in the morning quietness and stillness can produce so much more than rushing and racing. Your still time spent with the Lord resets you-the inner you. It reboots your patience and kindness. He also gives you joy and peace for any battle that might come your way. Even though you may feel as if you are doing nothing and not being productive enough, you are winning battles that you didn't even know were going on. Closeness to God helps defeat evil.

"May the Lord of peace Himself give you peace at all times and in every way. " -2 Thessalonians 3:16

June 6

Clay

Why do we try to force the potter's hand? Do we not trust his skill? If only for today, just be the moldable clay. Let him mold and shape you into what He wants and needs you to be.

"But now, O Lord Thou are our Father: we are the clay and Thou our potter, and we all are the work of Thy hand"- Isaiah 64:8

June 7

<u>God</u>

Ever heard people say why would God allow this…..God sees.

He sees everything.

He is so merciful and gracious that He wants none to perish. I am so glad that God doesn't use my human level of patience with people. Otherwise he would have said "That is it! I have had enough." a long time ago. But God in all his Godly ways shows mercy and patience and love in a way we cant humanly imagine. He is good and does good.

Jeremiah 23: 24

2 Peter 3:9

June 8

<u>**Our Children**</u>

As parents we pray for a lot for our children. One of my prayers for all my children is that they find that "perfect person". The person made just for them. This person encourages them, challenges them and makes them want to ne the best version of themselves. They love to talk to them, they truly understand them and love them fiercely. I hope and pray for this person for all my children. I want them to draw them closer to God and their purpose in this life.

Pray for your children. Pray for your spouse. Pray for your parents. Pray for your circle of friends. Pray for your pastor and your boss. Everyone needs prayer!

Don't know how to pray… No worries the Bible tells you.

The Lord's Prayer

Matthew 6:9-13

June 9

Tasked

Even the most menial task can bring joy to your creator.

Whatever you do, do it the best you possibly can.

Do it without grumbling or complaining.

Do it with joy as if you were doing it for your Father in Heaven.

"And Whatsoever ye do, do it heartily, as to the Lord, and not unto men; Knowing that of the Lord ye shall receive the reward of the inheritance: for ye serve the Lord Christ. "- Colossians 3:23-24

June 10

Awake at 2 AM

I just realized something. It just hit me square in the face. Those days that you are awakened at 2 AM, I think it is God wanting to wake you up to spend a little extra "alone time" with you. In my experience looking back, those are the days that might be a little more difficult. They might be a little more challenging. He knows you might need that extra time in prayer. Always bring glory to your creator in every situation. On those days you are awakened, go into prayer and ask the Lord to reveal what He has for you. And wait -

"Cause me to hear thy lovingkindness in the morning; For in thee do I trust: Cause me to know the way wherein I should walk; For I lift up my soul unto thee."- Psalm 143:8

June 11

Sunday is coming!

Have you heard the phrase "It might feel like Friday but your Sunday is coming?" Tough days happen sometimes. We go through tough seasons, but God is always there walking with you. God can use the difficult to make you better. He can give you great stories for opportunity to encourage someone else who might be going through the same. In the Christian life we know that Friday, the day Jesus was crucified and buried was a dark day. But we also rejoice because we know Sunday is coming- Sunday the day that Jesus was resurrected.

1 Peter 3:18-22

June 12

Live to the fullest

Make sure that you are enjoying your life. Take pictures, experience all the things. Put yourself out there and do the things that scare you. Tell people about Jesus and all He has done for you. Pray about situations that are not in your control. Change what you can and leave others better than you found them. Tell the ones you love how much they mean to you.

" Let us hold fast the profession of our faith without wavering; (for he is faithful that promised;) And let us consider one another to provoke unto love and to good works:"- Hebrews 10:23-24

June 13

What is important?

Make sure that you only have room in your life for things that you love, things that make you happy and things that are necessary. All of the rest are just distractions and are stealing your precious time. You have a limited time here on this earth, don't waste it on trivial things.

"Draw near to God and He will draw near to you."- James 4:8

June 14

He delighted in me

A few of my favorite verses, they get me right in the heart and speaks volumes to my soul. God has such love for us!

"But me he caught-reached all the way down from the sky to the sea; he pulled me out of that ocean of hate, that enemy chaos, the void in which I was drowning. They hit me when I was down, but God stuck by me. He stood me up on a wide- open field; I stood there saved- surprised to be loved!"- Psalm 18: 16-19 MSG

June 15

A puzzle

Ever been putting together a puzzle and as you get close to being finished you realize that you are missing a piece? A single piece makes all the difference. How disappointed and frustrating. Doing all that and still there is the void of the missing piece. Life is like that. You can get yourself together and try to do the best you can, but without that missing piece you aren't whole. God is that missing piece.

"God made my life complete when I placed all the pieces before him, When I got my act together, he gave me a fresh start. Now I'm alert to God's ways; I don't take God for Granted. Every day I review the ways he works; I try not to miss a trick. I feel put back together, and I'm watching my step. God wrote the text of my life when I opened the book of my heart to his eyes. "-Psalm 18: 20-24

June 16

God's Road

I love traveling. Sometimes there are parts of traveling that aren't as sweet. Curvy roads, bumpy roads give me car sickness. So my husband usually will ask which path we want to take; the straight roads or the curvy roads? Most times the curvy roads are faster. But is it really worth it? Getting there is half the fun with travel for me. In this life being a Christian isn't always easy. Sometimes those straight roads take a little bit longer. They aren't as much fun as the curvy roads , But it is worth it.

"What a God! His road stretches straight and smooth. Every God-direction is road-tested. Everyone who run toward him makes it"- Psalm 18:30 MSG

" Enter ye in at the straight gate: for wide is the gate and broad is the way, that leadeth to destruction, and many there be which go in thereat: Because straight is the gate, and narrow is the way, which leadeth unto life, and few there be that find it. " Matthew 7:13-14

June 17

Prayers

Ever woke up and just felt so good? You were like WOW! I know someone is praying for me. I certainly hope that is how my friends and family that I am praying for feel like as well. Pick a person for the next 30 days and pray for them. You don't have to tell them, just watch God work. It is amazing to see the difference your prayers make in the lives of those around us.

"So then you are no longer strangers and aliens, but you are fellow citizens with the saints and members of the household of God, built on the foundation of the apostles and the prophets, Christ Jesus himself being the cornerstone, in whom the whole structure, being joined together, grows into a holy temple in the Lord. In him also are being built together into a dwelling place for God by the spirit. "- Ephesians 2:19- 22

June 18

<u>Don't go at it alone</u>

We err if we try to do all the things on our own. Even while doing good things. Trust in God and his timing. We should stop trying so hard to make things happen. You should wait for God' leading. He will use your weakness to show his strength. Don't be impatient. Wait. Be happy knowing his timing is so much better. His ways are greater than our ways. Be excited in the anticipation of all he will do for and through you. You will not be disappointed.

"Whoever comes to me I will never cast out. For this is the will of my Father, that everyone who looks to the Son and believes in Him should have eternal life"- John 6: 37 and 40

" But without faith it is impossible to please him: for he that cometh to God must believe that he is, and that he is a rewarder of them that diligently seek him. "- Hebrews 11:6

"Kings will be your foster fathers, and their queens your nursing mothers. They will bow down before you with their faces to the ground; they will lick the dust at your feet. Then you will know that I am the Lord; those who hope in me will not be disappointed."- Isaiah 49:23 NIV

June 19

Answers

Being a Christian doesn't mean you always have all the answers or can explain everything from the Bible….(although sometimes you will), But it does mean that you have faith to believe without knowing all the why's. My standard answer when asked a question I don't know the answer to (and if you are my friend you know this to be true) is "That God's ways are higher than my ways and I don't understand it all right now but that one day I will."

Isaiah 55:5-9

June 20

Different

We all do life just a little differently. That is okay as long as you put God at the center of your life. Your life doesn't have less meaning because it doesn't look like your neighbor's or your pastor's life.

Make plans but let God direct your steps. Sometimes he will take you down a path that you least expected to go.

Don't think you have missed the mark because you are not where you planned or thought you would be, you are exactly where God wants you to be so he can use you.

"A man's heart deviseth his way; but the Lord directeth his steps" - Proverbs 16:9

June 21

Happy

If you expect to help someone else be happy; you have to be happy too. You can't teach something that you don't know anything about.

Love life. Enjoy every day. Find the good in everyday. Enjoy the time with those you love. When you truly appreciate all you have and stop focusing on the things lacking you will be happy. Happiness doesn't come from a pill or a bottle it is cultivated when you truly love your life even if it is less than perfect.

"Oh taste and see that the Lord is good; blessed is the man who trusts in him!"- Psalm 34:8

"Happy are the people whose God is the Lord"- Psalm 144:15

"Nothing is better for a man than he should eat and drink and that his soul should enjoy good in his labor. This also, I saw, was from the hand of God."- Ecclesiastes 2:24

June 22

<u>Rely on God</u>

Don't put trust in man or in man made things. Don't base your relationship with God on what you can do to "earn" his love. You will fall short every time. It's ok. It's not about what you can do but about what Jesus already did. Just accept it. Trust in it. No one can be disciplined enough. No one can do enough nice things. Our righteousness is like filthy rags. But thank God we are clothed in his righteousness.

"But we are all as an unclean thing, and all our righteousness are as filthy rags; and we all do fade as a leaf; and our iniquities, like the wind, have taken us away."- Isaiah 64:6

"I will rejoice greatly in the Lord, My soul will exult in my God; For He has clothed me with garments of salvation, He has wrapped me with a robe of righteousness, her jewels."- Isaiah 61:10

June 23

Lover of your soul

Remember God is the lover of your soul. He knows you more intimately than anyone else ever could.

He loves you unconditionally.

Revel in that love.

"But God demonstrated his own love for us in this: while we were still sinners, Christ died for us"-Romans 5:8

June 24

Sadness

Sometimes there are days where you are sad. There might not be a reason specifically but none the less you are sad. Embrace those days and cry. What I like to do is put on a tear jerker movie and cry. Let it out; but then move on. Don't stay in that same dark place. There are too many reasons for you to be happy. Sometimes through loss of someone or something we love our hearts get broken. There is a time to grieve. Observe that time. But think about what the person you lost would want you to do. Would they want you to be sad all the time? No. Would they want you to hide inside your home and not enjoy your life? No. Sometimes it honors the ones we lost if we become the things we loved so much in them. My Dad was an amazing Christian man. He loved to garden. He loved growing his own food. I enjoy that now. It helps me honor him and his memory. In the Bible, Jesus wept. Upon learning about Lazarus death Jesus wept. He knew he would be alive shortly but he still wept. He understood the feeling of loss. Even with Jerusalem Jesus wept out of compassion even though they were rejecting him and would eventually crucify him. Weeping is ok, even Jesus did it. But that wasn't all he did. Keep moving forward.

"Jesus wept"- John 11:35

"As he approached Jerusalem and saw the city, he wept over it and said "If you, even you, had only known on this day what would bring you peace-but now it is hidden from your eyes.""- Luke 19: 41-42

June 25

Closeness

Sometimes I pray for God to keep my kids and grandkids safe and close to Him. Close to God feels like the perfect place to be. When I want to make sure that my grandkids(or even my children when they were small) don't get lost I hold their hands and keep them close to me. I love that thought. I am asking Father God to hold their hands and keep them close to Him. You won't ever stray too far away as long as God is holding your hand. He can keep you close and safe.

June 26

Be Courageous

With God on your side you don't need to fear. If God is for you, who can be against you?

"Have I not commanded you? Be Strong and Courageous. Do not be frightened, do not be dismayed, for the Lord your God is with you wherever you go. "- Joshua 1:9

June 27

Peace

There are so many things happening in the world today. There is talk of wars, fighting, and lots of evil. There is trouble now but we know how this story ends. Don't get caught up on one part. Keep pressing on, fight the good fight. We know our peace does not come from the things of this world.

"I have said these things to you, that in me you may have peace. In the world you will have tribulation. But take heart; I have overcome the world. "- John 16:33

June 28

Worry

Worry just robs you of your joy for today. First things first, put God first and the rest will fall into place.

"So do not worry, saying "What shall we eat?" Or "what shall we drink? Or "what shall we wear?" For the pagans run after all these things, and your heavenly Father knows that you need them. But seek first His kingdom and His righteousness, and all these things will be given to you as well. Therefore do not worry about tomorrow, for tomorrow will worry about itself. Each day has enough trouble of it's own."- Matthew 6:31-34

June 29

Don't be selfish.

Ever been around selfish kind of people? It is all about them. No concern for anyone else. These people just have a "me, me, me" mentality. I can't say that I enjoy being around people like that.

"Do nothing from selfish ambition or conceit, but in humility count others more significant than yourselves. Let each of you look not only to his own interests, but also to the interests of others."- Philippians 2:3-4

June 30

Heaven

Do you just stop and think about Heaven some days? I do often. I wonder exactly how things will be. I look forward to there being no more pain or heartache. I look forward to seeing my loved ones again. I also look forward to seeing Jesus. I am so thankful for all He has done for me!

"He will wipe away every tear from their eyes, and death shall be no more, neither shall there be mourning or crying, nor pain anymore, for the former things have passed away." And He who was seated on the throne said "Behold, I am making all things new."- Revelation 21:4

July 1

Strength

Sometimes the very things that define strength are seen as weakness; such as silence, calmness and kindness. It takes a very strong person to remain calm and silent when others are waiting for a reaction. Kindness in the face of ridicule and persecution shows real strength. Don't let others decide how you will respond. Remain true to yourself. Your creator made you unique. Greater is he that is in you than he who is in the world. Your lack of response speaks volumes my friend.

"You are of God, little children and have overcome them: because greater is he that is in you, than he that is in the world"- 1John 4:4

July 2

Quiet

God's love is the only thing sometimes that can quiet our racing minds. His peace is the only thing that can comfort us at times. Don't worry. It was the way we were created. All is as it should be. Why don't you stop fighting and just rest in your creator's love and peace?

"The Lord thy God in the midst of thee is mighty; he will save, he will rejoice over thee with joy; he will rest in his love, he will joy over thee with singing."- Zephaniah 3:17

The NKJV is probably my favorite version of this verse.

" The Lord your God in your midst, The Mighty One, will save; He will rejoice over you with gladness, He will quiet you with His love, He will rejoice over you with singing"- Zephaniah 3:17 NKJV

July 3

Parents

Honor your parents. It is one of the commandments. There are consequences for not honoring them. I am so very blessed that my parents made it easy to honor them. For others, especially in abusive situations I know it can be a little more difficult.

"Honor your father and your mother, that your days may be long in the land that the Lord your God is giving you."- Exodus 20:12

July 4

Love

We each have our own way of expressing love. There are different levels of love. Love can come in many different forms. The Bible speaks a lot about love.

"We love because he first loved us"- 1John 4:19

"Love is patient, love is kind. It does not envy, it does not boast, it is not proud. It does not dishonor others, it is not self seeking, it is not easily angered, it keeps no record of wrongs. Love does not delight in evil but rejoices in the truth. It always protects, always trusts, always hopes, always perseveres. Love never fails."- 1 Corinthians 13:4-8

July 5

Distance

Sometimes those we love are separated from us either from distance or from death.

But we will be together again.

"The Lord watch between you and me, when we are out of one another's site"- Genesis 31:49

July 6

<u>God Cares</u>

Sometimes it gets pretty easy to think that because you have a small problem that God doesn't care. Well from reading about some of the miracles in the Bible, I don't believe that is true. You can read about the miracle where Jesus turns the water into wine because they ran out during a wedding celebration, proving that God cares for our needs. Also, this past Sunday our pastor talked about the floating ax head miracle and the fact that it was probably one of the most insignificant miracles in the Bible, but to the man that got the lost borrowed ax back, it was very significant. Again, this proves that God cares for all our needs even the ones that are small or might seem insignificant to some.

Read about the water into wine miracle John 2:1-11

Read about the floating ax head miracle in 2 Kings:1-7

July 7

<u>Perspective</u>

Our perspective shapes our perception. We all have things happen in life but our thoughts and the way we react to these things determine how they affect us.

Don't take yourself too seriously. Lighten up! Is this thing you are stressing about really gonna matter in 2 years? Don't waste your precious time on trivial issues that aren't gonna matter.

Philippians 4:8

July 8

<u>He knows</u>

God knows you.

You don't have to try to hide anything from him.

It is hard for us to truly understand unconditional love.

We think we know but we are only human.

We are fickle in our feelings.

Even though we try not to be some of our feelings are based on conditions.

1 Corinthians 13:12

July 9

Enemy

A lot of us are our own worst enemies. We judge the way we look in the mirror; from our gray hair to the extra weight on our hips and thighs. We say things to ourselves that we would never in a million years speak to another human being. Why?

We wouldn't say it because it isn't kind; in fact, it is harsh and cruel.

But we constantly speak this negativity to ourselves each day.

You are fearfully and wonderfully made by your creator.

July 10

Talk less, listen more

This one is difficult for me. I am from the south and being silent is hard for me. I always want to give my opinion (sometimes when it is not asked for). I never give my husband the silent treatment but am great at telling him exactly how I feel- all the time. During my quiet time with God it is also difficult for me to not try to fill this time with conversation. But I am learning sometimes when I am quiet I get so much more than when I am speaking. My driver's education teacher once told us girls you learn nothing with your mouth open. Which I know now he was telling us to talk less and listen more.

Proverbs 17:28

July 11

<u>Speak Life</u>

Choose the people very carefully that are in your circle.

Bad company can corrupt good character.

Choose to spend your time around life giving people.

Spend your time around people that speak positive things over you and encourage you to be better.

They say you can know your future by looking at the five people closest to you.

1 Corinthians 15:33

July 12

<u>God is with us</u>

God is always with us. God is there for every moment of our lives. Just because God doesn't show you what he has for you doesn't mean that he isn't equipping you for the journey. When we spend time with God he can prepare us for whatever our day or our journey might hold.

July 13

<u>It is ok to not be ok</u>

Don't pretend that everything is fine. You don't have to always have it all together.

It is through problems that God shows himself powerful. In our weakness he is made strong.

July 14

Only one you

Live the life God has for you. Everyone is on a different journey. God will equip you with what you need. Be thankful and grateful for the people in your life. You were created unique for your mission. There are several people whose lives are happier just because you are in it. Think of the people that you feel better just being around; those folks who encourage and inspire you. Who can you encourage and make happier? Be the reason someone doesn't give up!

July 15

Progress

I thank God that he doesn't require perfection from us, he only asks for progress. Just remember to make sure that you are moving forward. Just take small steps in the right direction and you will get to your destination. Slow and steady wins the race.

There will always be things to overcome but don't focus on the problems. Be joyful!

July 16

God's presence

God's presence in your life is the blessing. God is using your circumstances to draw you closer to him. Nothing can separate you from God's love.

You are not alone, during less than perfect circumstances he is walking closer than normal. You may not can see him but he is there.

God will always use the storm for your good.

July 17

To do lists

I am a list maker. I love to check things off my lists daily. Recently I was called out that my lists aren't what is important. A successful day isn't one that everything got checked off my list, it is one that I have remained in communication with God all day.

Make time for play as well, life isn't all about work. You can't pour from an empty cup. Get plenty rest and recharge. This will make your time at work so much more productive.

Sometimes things can wait!

July 18

Passion

What is your secret passion?

Is there something that ignites the fire in your soul?

Think about this. Pray about this.

Sometimes God puts desires in our heart that lead you to his purpose for your life.

July 19

Surprises

Do you approach your day with an expectation?

Are you excited to see what the day holds for you?

Treat each day like an adventure.

July 20

Be Bold

I wish that I could be bolder for Christ.

I pray about this being able to reach people for Jesus.

There is just something about a person who speaks confidently about God. Believing in God changes everything. We have to know that it is not about our human abilities. Just a little faith can move mountains!

Will you step out in your faith to help others meet Jesus?

Matthew 17:20

July 21

<u>Bloom where you are planted</u>

Many of us think if only I had this job or this house or that car I would be happy. Sorry to say but that is probably not accurate.

There will always be another job, another house or a different car that will call your name.

What if God wants to use you exactly where you are? What if he wants to put you in a different job but only after you have done what he needs you to at your current job? Sometimes you need to embrace where you are. Bloom and shine.

People that are happy carry themselves differently. Why don't you embrace that car? Sure, it has few extra miles but it is paid for. Maybe that house is a little small but it helps your family stay closer.

Bloom, shine the light of Jesus and forget about all the things that you want and think about all the things you have.

How very blessed you are.

July 21

<u>The Journey</u>

Life is not all about the destination but about the journey.

Enjoy getting there.

I always love car trips.

Sometimes the conversations and what happens on the way there is my favorite part. Those talks and all the laughing and jokes are priceless to me. I don't mind a few extra hours in the car. Being with the people in the car with me is exactly where I want to be anyway.

Don't look back and realize you were waiting to be happy until you got to your destination. Be happy in the now. Enjoy every day. Enjoy every part of the journey.

July 22

Roots

Trees whose roots are deep and strong don't need to fear the wind. If we are rooted and grounded in love we don't need to fear the storms of life either.

Make sure that you are firmly planted in the House of the Lord. Then you will have a steady supply of nourishment for your soul. You will flourish like a tree planted by the water.

Proverbs 11:28

Jeremiah 17:7-8

Ephesians 3:16-19

Psalm 92:12-13

July 23

Wonder of God

Don't ever lose the awe of the wonder of God. Fill your hearts with gratitude for all that He has done for you. See the daily miracles that others miss. Enjoy all the beauty in His creation. Appreciate and revel in his presence. Don't ever take his presence for granted.

"Let all the earth fear the Lord; Let all the inhabitants of the world stand in awe of him!

Hebrews 12:28-29

July 24

Quality time

My best days are the days that I wake up ready to spend time with Jesus. Spending quality time with Jesus prepares me for what my day holds; Whatever that might be.

For me to be truly happy, no matter what unpredictable things may happen, I need to have spent time with Jesus and centered myself on him.

If my eyes are on Jesus, there is no time to have my eyes on problems. Stay focused on the good.

July 25

Same Jesus

Jesus is the same. He hasn't changed. The Jesus that met the woman at the well, he is still the same Jesus that meets you where you are. The Jesus that healed the blind man, he is the same Jesus that can heal any of your ailments. The Jesus that calmed the storm, he is still the same Jesus and he can calm the storms of your life. We need to understand that the Jesus we read about in the Bible is that same Jesus that we are serving today. There is no limit to what He can do. Don't put limits on what God can do. Ask for those big things. He is a big God!

"Jesus Christ is the same yesterday and today and forever"- Hebrews 13:8

July 26

Making a Difference

There is so much joy that comes from knowing that you have made a difference in someone's life.

Sometimes you can make the biggest difference just by being available for people. Sometimes all people need is someone to listen to them.

Sometimes it is a kind gesture or just a helping hand. You will never know exactly how much your kindness meant to someone.

Try to help others if you can.

If you are financially blessed, share with those less fortunate. We are blessed to be a blessing. It is not about what you can acquire but those you can inspire.

Share the love of Jesus with others. Your kindness might make all the difference in a person's day.

July 27

Sheep

Sheep don't fear their shepherd. He protects them. He keeps them safe and looks after them. If one of them goes astray he leaves the group and goes to get it. How wonderful to have a caretaker that loves you this much.

We are his sheep.

"My sheep hear my voice, and I know them and they follow me: And I give unto them eternal life; and they shall never perish, neither shall any man pluck them out of my hand."- John 10:27-28

July 28

Past

Don't live in the past. Don't be satisfied in what happened in the past. Embrace the now. Embrace your future.

What will you do with today?

How will you give glory to your creator in your actions? Whatever lies ahead of you in this day bless the Lord.

Show those you encounter His love.

July 29

As if for the Lord

Honor the Lord in whatever you do.

If you are a surgeon, be the best surgeon you can be.

If you clean houses clean as if it were for the Lord.

If you are a housewife, care for your family as if it were for the Lord.

If you empty trash, be the best trash man ever; do everything you do, do it the best you can as if it were for the Lord and not for man.

Colossians 3:23-24

July 30

Trust the process

I enjoy doing the painting videos. I enjoy them mostly because you don't have to have any artistic ability. The person who is leading the video has all the instructions you need. While doing one of these with my daughter, Leilani, (who is very artistic) and my Mother, I was getting a little frustrated at how my painting was looking. I couldn't see where we would end up but my daughter said something to me that has stuck with me. She said trust the process Mom. How powerful is that! In a sense she was telling me that even though I couldn't see what I was creating the person leading the class knew how it would all turn out. Do you know what? She was absolutely correct. I actually LOVE my painting I did that day. I stopped stressing so much about what I couldn't see and listened to her instructions and followed her lead. This can be related to our walk with the Lord. We don't know everything about the details but if we trust the process, stay close to the one that does it will turn out beautiful. A masterpiece! It's not about my plans but following his direction for my life that leads to the magic.

Proverbs 3:5-6

July 31

Shift your perspective

Have you ever had something happen that shifted your perspective immediately? While traveling late at night on a small back road I had a deer jump out in front of me and only by the grace of God I missed it. I can tell you after that there was no other thing as important to me as getting home safely. Sometimes we have so many cares and worries going on that we really aren't present. When we have something bring us back to reality so shocking the important things overshadow all the little minute daily issues.

Don't sweat the small stuff- remember it's all really small stuff!

August 1

Detours

Sometimes our direction of travel gets diverted. This can happen literally and figuratively. I remember back to a church trip that we were on. There were a couple of vans traveling together. The person driving the van that I was in knew the way there. But our driver took the wrong road and I remember he was very surprised and joking around with the other van driver that he had missed his turn and we turned around at a new station parking lot and headed back to our correct road. What we didn't know at that moment was that there was a HUGE wreck that had taken place and had he taken the correct road, we would have been right there and probably involved in it as well. That has always stuck with me. Sometimes God uses detours to get us safely to our destinations. These detours are not always convenient and sometimes we don't understand. Sometimes we are upset at the delay not knowing what we are being protected from.

"For he shall give his angels charge over thee, to keep thee in all thy ways. They shall bear thee up in their hands, lest thou dash thy foot against a stone." - Psalms 91: 11-12

August 2

Branch out

Do you feel stuck in the same ole rut? I don't believe we were created to live a boring dull mediocre life. Shake things up. Try something new. Do new things. Don't be happy with mediocre lives. Live each day to the fullest. Live. You might find new passions in the unknown. Maybe you will unlock the inner painter or singer. Maybe you will try something new and realize that it is your calling. How exciting it is to branch out. Do not fear the unknown.

"I will instruct you and teach you in the ways you should go; I will guide you with My eye."- Psalm 32:8

August 3

Road less traveled

Sometimes we need to be reminded we were called to a road less traveled. It is not glamorous all the time. No ticker tape parades are had in your honor. In doing what God has for you; you are making the greatest difference. I am so thankful and feel blessed God uses me for his purposes even if right now I can't see exactly the difference it is making.

Dig into these scriptures and let them get into your soul.

Proverbs 3:5-6; 16-20

Jeremiah 29:11

John 15:5

Isaiah 49:13

James 1:4

August 4

Listen with His ears

Do you ask God to help you listen to others and really hear what they sometimes aren't saying? I do. I pray for God to give me ears to hear and to also give me what I should say. Sometimes, I have no idea what to respond with. How much better our responses and our advice could be if we were to use God's filters to respond. Really listen and wait for what the Holy Spirit would instruct you to respond with. Some of us have a gift of being a good listener to other's problems. Could we not also be a good listener to God and wait for the Holy Spirit before we respond?

The next time someone comes to you, try to really listen to them and wait before you respond.

August 5

Carry on

Here lately folks have shocked me.

But even if people shock us or say hurtful things; carry on.

Do you.

You can't control peoples actions, but you can control how you respond.

Be wise, keep your wits about you but still be kind.

The mistake people make sometimes is they perceive your kindness for weakness, but it is not weakness.

It takes a strong person to remain kind in an unkind, self serving world. Greater is he that lives in you chica.

You are a child of the King.

Straighten that crown.

Persevere.

Hebrews 12:1

August 6

Never too far gone

There is no road that takes you too far that you can't turn around. God never forces anyone to come to him. He beckons you, but He also gave you free will. You will never accidently end up a Christian. It is a choice; a personal decision that you must make for yourself. No one can decide for you. He stands at the door and knocks but he never comes in until you invite him.

"Behold, I stand at the door, and knock: if any man hear my voice, and open the door, I will come in to him, and will sup with him and he with me."

Revelations 3:20

August 7

God's protection

There is not a limit to what God can do. You have a God of angel armies on your side. You need not fear. It is great to think that God would leave the ninety-nine to come rescue you. When you feel like you have nothing left, let him carry you. He is a protector. He can fight your battles for you. He cares for you more than you can imagine. He knows how many hairs are on your head and he has all your tears in a bottle. You are his. Rest in that.

"He shall cover thee with his feathers, and under his wings shalt thou trust: his trust shall be thy shield and buckler. "- Psalms 91:4

August 8

<u>Life marches on</u>

Even when you have had the worst day or experience of your life, just keep in mind, life still marches on.

Sometimes we want to stop the crazy train and get off, but that isn't the way life works.

Look up child.

Don't let the bad days win.

With God's help you can figure it out.

God is still in control. That doesn't mean that you won't need some time to get away from it all and be still. I have found sometimes the greatest therapy is just to get away, turn off all distractions and be silent and still.

August 9

<u>God loves us</u>

God is our safe space. He can be our anchor or our rock. His love is never ending and not based on anything that you do or have done. It is hard for us as humans to truly understand the depth of his love. The scriptures below are some of my favorites and speak volumes to me. They always make me instantly feel better and so loved.

"But me he caught- reached all the way from the sky to sea; he pulled me out of that ocean of hate, that enemy of chaos, the void in which I was drowning.

They hit me when I was down but God stuck by me.

He stood me up on a wide open field; I stood: there saved-Surprised to me loved"

-Psalms 18:16-19 MSG

August 10

Goodness of God

I can look back on my life and see just how good God has been to me. In times when I didn't deserve to be loved, God showered me with love and blessings. He has never left me even when I walked away from him. Even when my circumstances might not be ideal, it does not change how good God is. He is Holy and in him is no evil.

"The Lord is good, a refuge in times of trouble. He cares for those who trust in Him"- Nahum 1:7

August 11

Be an encourager

You were created differently. God has given you a gift. You bring light and happiness to a room. Use your gift to encourage others along the way. Not everyone sees the world like you do. They need you to share your outlook to help them in times of trouble. Sometimes all it takes is a word of encouragement to change someone's path. Spread love and life where you go. Be the reason someone believes again.

You never know what those you encounter are going through. You may make all the difference in their life.

Speak life.

August 12

Dry your tears

There is a time for everything under the heavens, even sadness. But that is only for a season. Put away your sorrows. Step into his goodness. We are over comers. We serve the God of Abraham. He is the Alpha and the Omega. Our heartache is not the end. God is still writing your story. Sometimes we have to turn the page to get to our happy ending. When we put our faith in Jesus he will never let us down. We can have a peace that makes no sense to the world.

"There failed not ought of any good thing which the Lord had spoken unto the house of Israel; all came to pass. "- Joshua 21:45

Ecclesiastes 3:1

August 13

Just keep going

God is depending on you to do your best for him.

Keep going.

Don't quit, even when it is hard and you feel like you have nothing left to give.

People are watching you and waiting for you to give up. Make them wonder what keeps you going and make them wonder what is different about you.

Decide that today you are going to live from your heart and not give in even if it is hard at times.

August 14

Prepare for your miracle

Have you been praying for a miracle?

Are you living in expectation of that miracle?

Do you speak as if it is certain?

Don't let doubt steal your miracle from you.

If you are praying for a baby, are you preparing a room?

Trust God and live in expectation of him keeping his promises. The devil knows he only has to make you doubt God. He is a liar and in him is no truth.

Stand on the promises of God and you will see your miracle come to pass.

August 15

Abundance

God is a God of abundance.

He will never run out of resources.

Don't be afraid to ask him for big things.

We serve a mighty God. Doing something mighty for you does not take away what he can do for others.

He is limitless.

Approach him with high expectations.

Don't limit your prayers because God can do anything! As my pastor says, "More for you, is not less for someone else."

Deuteronomy 28: 47-48

Roman 12:11

August 16

<u>God see's you</u>

God knows exactly where you are.

He understands you.

There is not the need to sugar coat with God.

He wants you to come to him with it all; the ugly, the messy.

You don't need to pick the perfect words or tone it down for God.

Pour out your hearts to him.

We are so used to shielding those around us from the parts that aren't ideal.

We are used to only showing the good things and keeping the" b roll" quality to deal with on our own.

God already knows. Don't hold back.

There is no need. He knows you better than you know yourself.

August 17

<u>Friends are important</u>

Stay away from toxic people. Spend time with people who speak life into your situation. The people you spend the most time with are your battle buddies. Can you count on them? Are they lifting you up in prayer? Are you lifting them up in prayer? Be the kind of friend you want. Life is busy. Daily conversations aren't necessary but check in on those in your circle. Cover them in prayer. Help each other through the tough times because it happens to us all.

"For if they fall, the one will lift up his fellow: but woe to him that is alone when he falleth for he hath not another to help him up" - Ecclesiastes 4:10

August 18

<u>Mistakes</u>

We all make mistakes.

It is not the end all be all.

If you own your mistakes, and learn from your mistakes they are not in vain.

Remember no one is perfect.

God doesn't require perfection just progress.

August 19

<u>Self care</u>

It is important to make sure you get enough rest.

Even God thought that rest was important as we know that on the seventh day he rested.

You can't pour from an empty cup.

 Get enough rest and also eat right.

These are things that increase your happiness.

August 20

<u>Checklists</u>

Stop worrying about your checklists so much.

You don't have to feel like a failure if you aren't checking all the boxes in a day. Did you have communication with the Father? If so, you have had a successful day. It is ok if you leave a few things on your daily checklists.

One of my friends has a rule for herself. If she completes at least 3 things on her daily list she is happy with her day. The main thing is to not set unrealistic goals for yourself and then feel bad when you don't reach them. Small accomplishments are still accomplishments.

August 21

<u>Perspective</u>

I often hear folks talk negatively about the self check out registers questioning why they have to check themselves out saying things like "I don't work here".

I love them. I choose to think that I get to bag my own groceries like I like them. I get to take my time. Plus it is a choice. No one is being forced.

Just like other folks complaining about "having to go to work". I think I get to go to work.

So many people wish they had a dependable job. It's all about perspective.

Shift your perspective just a little and you will see things very differently.

It will change your life.

August 22

<u>Search me</u>

My prayer for today was that God would help me see others as he sees them, even when they might not be kind to me or they do things that frustrate me. I pray that He would help me to be more like Jesus every day.

My Pastor covered the fact that if we truly had the fear of the Lord we would be very careful of the way that we treat others. That it would bother us to treat others unkindly and that we should want to rid ourselves of any bitterness, hard feelings or any other things that could come between the relationship we have with Him. Boy that sermon really touched me. Sometimes I am so guilty of this. I let the way people act and treat me set the tone for how I feel about them; when in fact, I should love them like Jesus loves them. It's hard. I'm not going to lie; it is a work in progress for me.

"Search me, O God, and know my heart; test me and know my thoughts. Point out anything in me that offends You, and lead me along the path of everlasting life." - Psalm 139: 23-24

August 23

Everyday life

Rejoice in the everyday things of life. Enjoy every moment that you get. Decide to be happy. Fix your thoughts on good things. Even problems, don't run from them. Sometimes these issues are hand tailored for you. They are opportunities for God to bless you and increase your faith.

"I have said these things to you, that in me you may have peace. In the world you will have tribulation. But take heart; I have overcome the world." - John 16:33

August 24

What?

What is holding you back from being what God wants you to be?

What will it take for you to lay it down?

What do you need to remove out of your life?

I suggest that you ask God to reveal these things to you. Think about if it is truly worth hanging on to. Is it worth your happiness? Are you going to let it possibly keep you out of Heaven?

"But the fruit of the Spirit is love, joy, peace, longsuffering, gentleness, goodness, faith, meekness, temperance: against such there is no law. " - Galatians 5:22-23

August 25

Stand

Stand your ground when you are standing for God and good.

Remember that God uses what was meant for evil for our good.

We serve a powerful mighty God.

Don't fear your limitations or measure the day's demands against your strength. If God allows it to come to you He will equip you to get through it.

"Have not I commanded thee? Be strong and of a good courage; be not afraid, neither be thou dismayed: for the Lord thy God is with thee whithersoever thou goest."- Joshua 1:9

Hebrews 13:20-21

August 26

<u>Abundance</u>

Does your life speak that you have abundance?

I am not talking about financial things.

Are you living each day to its fullest?

Are you flourishing?

Does your happiness make others want some of what you have?

God is a God of abundance. He never asks you to give up anything that you won't be abundantly blessed for.

"I came that they may have life and have it abundantly."- John 10:10

August 27

<u>Joyful</u>

Be joyful.

Don't worry, worship.

Remember that God is always faithful to us!

He is always there.

Faith, as small as a mustard seed, can move mountains.

"And let us not grow weary of doing good, for in due season we will reap, if we do not give up."- Galatians 6:9

August 28

<u>Words</u>

Your mouth is a powerful weapon.

Words can lift or destroy others.

Choose your words wisely.

Speak life building, kind encouraging words.

"Gracious words are like a honeycomb, sweetness to the soul and health to the body."- Proverbs 16:24

Proverbs 29:19-20

August 29

<u>Brave</u>

God's love makes us brave.

There is nothing like God's presence.

It steadies us.

His love and His presence strengthens us.

Not that any of us have done anything to deserve his love, but He freely gives it to us, unconditionally.

"My soul clings to you; your right hand upholds me."- Psalm 63:8

Psalm 37:23-24

1 Samuel 30:6

August 30

<u>**Anxiety**</u>

Anxiety is toxic.

It creates worry and fear.

These are things that God has said not to do.

Cast your cares on Him.

He cares for you.

I have often heard that the best way to forget about your own problems is to help someone else through theirs.

It is said it is better to give than to receive.

Remember: It can wait- take a deep breath!

"For God hath not given us the spirit of fear; but of power, and of love, and of a sound mind."- 2 Timothy 1:7

August 31

<u>**Music and song**</u>

Music can boost your mood.

I have my own little concert on the way to work in my car.

There is just something about belting out some lyrics.

Now don't get me wrong, I can't hold a tune; But that tiny little detail doesn't stop me.

Music just speaks to our soul. Especially worship music.

Psalms 96

Colossians 3

Ephesians 5:19

"Sing aloud unto God our strength: Make a joyful noise unto the God of Jacob."- Psalm 81:1

September 1

Celebrate

What a great word.

To celebrate means to acknowledge an event with a social gathering or an enjoyable activity.

Throwing a party, would be an example of a type of celebration.

What are you celebrating today?

Celebration is what gets you through the hard days.

Rejoice and be glad in this day.

Celebration doesn't have to be only large events.

You can celebrate the most common moments as long as they bring you joy. Be thankful. Be joyful.

Celebrate!

Remember that your worship celebrates what God has done for you.

Psalm 118

September 2

Pray for people

Sometimes the most powerful thing you can do for a person is lift them up in prayer. There are so many things that people are going through that we know nothing about. God knows. If you see a friend struggling, pray for them. If you know they have had a bad week, pray for them. If you know they have had a good week, pray for them. Pray that it continues for them. See an ailment in their body pray for healing. Jesus said that we would do even greater things. But we have to ask. Seek and you will find. Are you looking for miracles? Are you praying in expectation?

"Verily, verily, I say unto you, He that believeth on me, the works that I do shall he do also; and greater works than these shall he do; because I go unto my Father."- John 14:12

September 3

Unique

No two days are alike.

They might have similar occurrences but each is different. We wake up and start our day not knowing what is going to happen along the way. But, we can make sure that we are ready for whatever the day holds if we first start our day with some alone time with God. Make sure that you have a place that is ideal. I use my kitchen table, but I choose to have my quiet time when the rest of the house is sleeping. This means that I get up a little earlier. It is well worth the missed sleep. Make sure you don't have any distractions. If you choose to play worship music, this is not a distraction. Even though it might not be quiet it is ushering in His presence through the worship songs.

I make myself a cup of coffee grab my bible and my devotional books and sit. I like to call this "My Still time with God".

September 4

Represent Jesus

Sometimes there are people that have no desire to have peace with you. You can try everything possible and they will always find fault with you. Make sure that your desire to be right is always behind your desire to represent Jesus. For some people your life is the only sermon they will ever hear. Try to remember what Jesus would do. Jesus wasn't liked by everyone and I am sorry to tell you that you won't be either. But you can still be nice to people that don't like you. Pray for them; go out of your way to do kind things for them. It speaks volumes to them when you do this. People who haven't experienced God's love first hand usually can't understand this. Let them experience Jesus love through your kindness.

September 5

Worship

I love going to church. It refreshes me and encourages me. There is just something powerful about gathering corporately to worship God. I love when God's presence is so strong that you can sense it in every aspect of the service. There is just nothing else that compares to this. I am so very thankful that during Covid lockdowns that our church as still able to have online services. And now and again situations arise where we have to watch online but I would encourage you to be in church if you can. I know some of you can only attend online. There is nothing that compares to being there in person. God can meet you wherever you are, but worshipping with other believers is powerful.

"Not forsaking the assembling of ourselves together, as the manner of some is; but exhorting one another: and so much the more, as ye see the day approaching."- Hebrews 10:25

September 6

<u>Rapture</u>

Anyone else ever dream of the rapture? I do quite often. Every time I have the dream it stays with me for a while. I hear the trumpet-I feel my body go weightless and start to lift up. There is fear and excitement mixed every time. Can you imagine the fear for those that don't know the Lord? That day will be the beginning of a lot of fear for those who have not accepted Jesus Christ as their personal savior. We should be busy about spreading the word so that everyone has the opportunity to come to know Jesus. What will you do today to share Christ with the world?

"I came that they may have life and have it abundantly."- John 10:10

September 7

<u>Good Gifts</u>

Are you a good gift giver? There are certain times of the year when people feel obligated to give gifts. Some of these events but certainly not all are birthdays, Christmas, weddings, anniversaries, for a house warming, baby showers and the list goes on and on. Some people get so very stresses out at this task. We want to get the perfect gift. Remember, not everything that is a great gift has to have a price tag. Gifts of service, kind deeds or a card with some encouraging words are perfect gifts and cost nothing but your time and effort. Being available to some and willing to help are all priceless and mean so much to others. It is ok to ask someone what they need. We should be more about filling a need of a person than just checking buying a present off of our list.

James 1:17

September 8

Gods timing

God's timing is perfect.

Sometimes the waiting is hard.

I'll admit it. I am a very impatient person.

We don't know the whole story or see the big picture but God does.

Trust him today in the waiting.

God loves you greater than anyone ever could. He has great plans for you. Remember, His timing, not yours.

Romans 8:28

September 9

Stillness

What is it about stillness that can be so refreshing? Quieting the mind helps to energize the soul. Peace is so very important. Don't sweat the small stuff in life. Make sure that you focus on the important things.

"As members of one body you are all called to live in peace. And always be thankful."- Colossians 3:15

September 10

Loss

I lost my Dad a couple years ago. One of the things that makes me sad is all the things that we can't share with him. It breaks my heart that he won't see my youngest daughter graduate or get married and start a family. He won't get to see his Grandson get married or start a family. It breaks my heart that he can't see his great grandkids grow. He loved them so much and when I see them change I hate that he isn't here to be a part of that. Loss is real. It is different for everyone. And everyone has those things that cause it to resurface. Even Jesus wept. Don't keep it all inside. Feel all your emotions. Don't try to repress them. We don't always have to be happy. I'm not sure I have ever met someone that has always been happy. We all have sad days. The thing to remember is that we can't live there. Enjoy life. If for no other reason, enjoy the rest of your life for the ones that you have lost.

"Pour out your hearts to Him, for God is our refuge."- Psalm 62:8

September 11

Sadness

As I sit here and remember events that took place on this day in 2001. I remember the feeling of fear; feelings that I had no idea what was happening and that I had no control. But, I also remember the closeness that happened to our country. This single event reminded us all that we are all connected. We are all human, I remember all that meant at that time. We were all in it together.

I miss that unity.

"I appeal to you, brothers and sisters, in the name of our Lord Jesus Christ, that all of you agree with one another in what you say and there be no divisions among you, but that you be perfectly united in mind and thought."- 1 Corinthians 1:10

September 12

<u>**A better Christian**</u>

If you read my prayer journal you would see I often pray, "Lord help me be a better Christian." What is that exactly? Does that mean I am asking to be perfect? No. What that means to me is help me Lord to reflect your love as I am stuck in traffic or dealing with someone who is less than kind. It means help me Lord to get up early to steal away to study your word even though I might be tired because it is good for my soul. It means help me each day to have a little less of me and a little more of you Lord. It also means to help me to forgive others as you have forgiven me. It means for me to pause before I respond and ask myself is what I am about to say true, kind and necessary? And if I answer no to any of those things help me to stay quiet. Being a Christian we are to strive to be a "little Christ". I strive for that daily and most days come up short. I know I will never be perfect but with His help I can get closer to Him every day.

"Be Kind to one another, tenderhearted, forgiving one another, even as God in Christ forgave you."- Ephesians 4:32

September 13

Marriage

I believe God blesses the union of marriage. I think he expects to be at the center of your marriages though. I often pray for my marriage. We should pray for our partners. If you aren't married or even if you are single, pray for your future partners. Life is difficult sometimes for everyone. Praying for your spouse or your partner just helps them along their way. I certainly hope my spouse prays for me. I have some scriptures below about marriage and love. Read them. Study them and see how you can use them to strengthen your marriage and your bond with your spouse.

Genesis 2:24

Ephesians 5:25

1 Corinthians 7: 3-11

1 Corinthians 13:4-7

Amos 3:3

Proverbs 18:27

Mark 10:9

Ephesians 4:2

1 John 4:12

September 14

Human

Have you ever just stopped to think about the human body? Are you amazed at how God thought of everything? I am so amazed thinking about everything from a yawn to a hiccup, all the organs and veins and all their functions and how everything has its own purpose. Just think about the complexity of all the inner working of your body. Think about all the things that work together in such a way so that you are you. You are so complex. God created all of that and yet he knows you so well that he knows exactly how many hairs are on your head. It amazes me at how complex and yet how personal.

"Thank you for making me so wonderfully complex! Your workmanship is marvelous- and how well I know it." Psalm 139:14

"But even the very hairs of your head are all numbered. Fear not therefore: ye are more valuable than many sparrows." - Luke 12:7

September 15

Looking and seeing

These are two very different things. You can look but not see. Ever had a friend tell you that they saw you the other day and you have no idea what they are talking about? Sometimes they even say you were looking right at me. I have had this happen so many times. I might have been looking in their direction but never saw them. We have to make sure that we stop just looking and start seeing. Start seeing all the blessings of God on your life. See Jesus in the random situations in your day. Slow down if you need to but make an effort to stop just looking, start to see.

"Looking unto Jesus the author and finisher of our faith; who for the joy that was set before him endured the cross, despising the shame, and is set down at the right hand of the throne of God"- Hebrews 12:2

"The light of the body is they eye: if therefore thine eye be single, thy whole body shall be full of light. But if thine eye be evil, thy whole body shall be full of darkness. If therefore the light that is in thee be darkness, how great is that darkness!"- Matthew 6:22-23

September 16

<u>Perception</u>

Our perspective shapes our perception. We all have hard things happen in life but our thoughts about these things determine how they affect us. It is not necessary what is happening to you but how you respond and how you look at your situation. Have you seen the picture of two people on the train the one is looking out their window and seeing the sun and a beautiful view and the other is seeing the mountain side that is dark and covered in rocks- they are both on the same train but one has a very different outlook than the other. That is life. It is all about choices and how we are going to view the things that happen to us.

"Rejoicing in hope; patient in tribulation; continuing instant in prayer;"

Romans 12:12

September 17

Thankful

Do you wake up thankful? Are you thankful for another day? Are you thankful for another chance? We need to live life to the fullest. Have a grateful, thankful heart. I often say this but what if you only had today what you thanked God for yesterday? We should be a people who are so very thankful. We have so many blessings that we take for granted. You should be thankful if: you have a relationship with Jesus Christ, you have clean water, if you live in America, if you have a roof over your head and a nice bed to sleep, if there is food in your fridge and you have loved ones around you, if you drive your own car to work, if you have a job, if your parents are still alive, you have grandkids, you have a loving spouse, you have wonderful children and this list could go on and on. I am so very grateful and thankful for all my blessings. I realize that so many others are not as blessed and still they are thankful. It is ok to be known as the one who goes on and on about how thankful and blessed you are.

"I will give thanks to the Lord with my whole heart; I will recount all of your wonderful deeds. I will be glad and exult in you; I will sing praise to your name O Most High." - Psalm 9:1-2

September 18

Company

Who you hang around with has a direct effect on you. Make sure that you are deciding to be around friends that are positive and uplifting. Negativity is more contagious than the common cold. If you are around people who are always negative it starts to rub off on you before you even know it. Before you know it, you are the negative one. I have always heard that misery loves company. And if you think you can change them for the better, well I sure hope that you are "prayed up" and have had alone time with God and an extra cup of coffee before you are around them for too long. You will need a constant refreshing of positivity in order to come out of it.

"Bad company corrupts good character"- 1 Corinthians 15:33

September 19

Worry

Isn't it nice to know that you will never run out of things to worry about? There is an infinite amount of things that could happen and things that could go wrong. But there is the same amount of good things that could happen as well. It is all about what you are going to focus on. They say that majority of things we worry about never happen. What a waste of your precious time. If we worry it shows our lack of faith in God.

"Be careful for nothing; but in everything by prayer and supplication with thanksgiving let your requests be made known to God. And the peace of God, which passeth all understanding, shall keep your hearts and minds through Christ Jesus."- Philippians 4:6-7

September 20

Love without Boundaries

Love is in the details. God loves you so much! When you reach Heaven and you see how your whole life was stitched together with so much love and how he was orchestrating everything to get you to where he needed you - you will be amazed!

Try something today. Count your blessings! Count all the things that make you so very happy. Count all the people who love you so very much. Don't forget to count all the wonderful things that you look forward to. Whether it be that first cup of coffee or that furry little guy that meets you at the door every day. If you stop to count your blessings you will soon find out that you don't have time to worry about all the things that you don't have.

God is so good, and He is good all the time.

"That Christ may dwell in your hearts by faith; that ye, being rooted and grounded in love, May be able to comprehend with all saints what is the breadth, and length, and depth, and height. And to know the love of Christ, which passeth knowledge, that ye might be filled with all the fullness of God." Ephesians 3:17-19

September 21

<u>Be light</u>

Don't bring doom and gloom where you go.

Be the sunshine.

We as Christians should be so happy and joyful that others want to know what's the secret, then you can tell them about Jesus.

It's all because of Jesus.

Is there still problems? Of course, but he carries the burdens; he walks with you and you are never alone.

How wonderful is his companionship.

September 22

<u>People</u>

People will let you down. Sometimes even shock you by their behavior. No one is perfect. Don't place others on a pedestal. Only God should hold that position. People are only human. They make human mistakes. Even the best of people are not perfect. Keep this in mind as you go about your days. If you are looking for perfection, God is the only place to find it.

Don't place your hope in man; you will be disappointed every time.

Psalms 118: 8-14

September 23

<u>Who is Jesus?</u>

I would suggest you read the whole chapter of Matthew and you will see Jesus is so many things. He is kind. He is strong. He is patient. He is forgiving. He loves you. He is righteous and holy. He heals and redeems.

But who is Jesus to you? Is He a friend? Are you walking with Him? Are you talking to Him?

"Come unto me, all ye that labour and are heavy laden, and I will give you rest. Take my yoke upon you, and learn of me; for I am meek and lowly in heart: and ye shall find rest unto your souls. For my yoke is easy, and my burden is light." Matthew 11:28-30

September 24

<u>Not much</u>

Aren't you so happy that all God really wants is our heart.

He doesn't require any fancy titles or skills.

He just wants your heart.

Your gratitude and praise means so much to Him.

And you know the best thing about this? It costs nothing to worship Him.

He loves to hear your voice.

Praise is so powerful.

Wherever you are right now, throw up your hands and praise Him. It's priceless and so powerful!

September 25

<u>Death</u>

Have you ever just thought about a cemetery? They are always so gray and gloomy. I remember when my youngest daughter was little, I told her I wanted my tombstone to be yellow-like the sun. I said that I wanted people to look at that and be happy. See the happy life I had. When my Dad passed away a couple years ago my daughter and I painted my Dad's tombstone. It was beautiful. It had color and was bright and made me smile when I saw it. My Dad's not there in that spot. I know this. He is with Jesus in Heaven, but that is somewhat of a representation of him. Why not make it beautiful? Let's vow to look at death differently.

September 26

Kind things

Why do we wait until someone leaves a job or dies to say kind things? Give people their flowers while they are still here.

If you think something is amazing about someone, tell them! Talk about how they make your life better. Don't wait until it is too late to tell them how wonderful you think they are.

September 27

Nature's beauty

Do you notice the beauty around you? I am one of those people that take pictures of the sunrise (I take picture of everything really). It is amazing. I am always amazed at the beauty. I hope I never get to a point to where I don't appreciate the beauty around me. Trees, flowers, ponds if you take the time to notice, beauty is everywhere. Appreciate God's creation. It's ok to be "that person". Secretly, I think everyone is anyway, they just don't admit it .

September 28

Calming

Have you ever been around someone that just had a calming spirit? My husband's Aunt Gwen was that person. She spoke softly and you always felt better after talking to her. She just had a calming sense about her. She really talked to you and had wonderful meaningful conversations. She was truly present and made you feel heard. She was such a wonderful Godly woman. People like Gwen change the world in a gentle way.

September 29

<u>Get away</u>

Ever felt that you just needed to get away from everything? We all feel this way sometimes. Sometimes I just want to be alone with my thoughts. No phone, no television, no music or sound of any kind. It is a different time that when I was growing up. Back then, there weren't cell phones, we weren't surrounded by technology. It all gets to be too much at times and we need to unplug. We are exposed to the constant videos or photos of people who are beautiful and seem to have it all together. We put too much pressure on ourselves to measure up. When in actuality, the photos are edited and you only get to see the pretty. We all have the photos that we don't share and we all have down days. It is ok to get away.

I suggest spending some time alone in prayer. It helps me. Whether that time is before you go to bed or when you get up. Your alone time might be in your car on your way home. How and where don't matter as much as you making it a priority.

September 30

<u>Generosity</u>

When we help other folks it makes us happier. That is why we always hear it is better to give than to receive. It just feels good to give. If you can help someone, make sure that you do. Help others even, if it isn't something huge and groundbreaking. It is the little things in life that determine the big things.

"A generous person will prosper; whoever refreshes others will be refreshed" - Proverbs 11:25

"His lord said unto him, well done, thou good and faithful servant: thou hast been faithful over a few things, I will make thee ruler over many things: enter thou into the joy of thy lord." - Matthew 25:21

October 1

Time

I don't mind telling you that I am not patient.

I am not proud of this fact, but it is simply truth. I want things done quickly. I even walk fast. I want immediate results. Like when I start to diet for weight loss. I want to see immediate results. Good things take time. Not everything is instantaneous. Celebrate the process every day. Enjoy getting there. Don't waste a single day. Set a goal for yourself and start. You can't win if you don't begin. It won't happen overnight but it will happen. And if you stray from your goal be teachable in your spirit and get back to it. God knows and loves you even if you miss the mark sometimes. Think about small steps and celebrate small victories and before long you will have reached your goal.

October 2

Lenses of love

Stop and think about how much could be avoidable if we only looked at others through lenses of love. What if we saw others as Jesus does? Would we care so much about petty things? Wouldn't it be a little easier to show others grace? I am so glad that God doesn't just see all my shortcomings when he looks at me. Because of Jesus, and me being covered with His righteousness, I get to look spotless to him. Why can't we think about this when we are looking at others and just show a little mercy? If not for their sake, do it for yours.

Jesus banner that hangs over me is love.

Let's share that.

Let's treat others as we want to be treated.

And think about how Blessed we are!

October 3

Delegate

I have learned that I cannot do everything alone.

Sometimes you have to delegate.

Delegation is not a bad thing.

Share the tasks. Share the burdens.

We were not created to be alone or do everything alone. It does not make you less of a person to admit that you need help.

Sometimes it is just nice to share the load; especially the tasks that are uninspiring but that never the less still need to get done.

October 4

Seek God first

God tells us that if we seek him first that all other things will be given to us but He needs to be first.

If God is for us, who can be against us? We always talk about friends having our back or being our "ride or die"- how awesome would it be if we looked to God for that? Ultimately He is. Let's work on our relationship with God so that we are so close in our walk with Him, that He is the first and who we depend on the most. God is infinite.

"Seek first the kingdom of God and his righteousness, and all these things will be added to you"- Matthew 6:33

"If God be for us who can be against us?" - Romans 8:31

October 5

Laugh

It's best to not take yourself too seriously. You should laugh at yourself often. Be lighthearted.

Overlook some minor things for the happiness of your family. Jesus knows all your faults and still loves you anyway. Don't let simple inconveniences ruin your day.

We get 24 brand new, fresh hours every day.

It is completely up to us how we will spend them.

How are you going to make this day count for His kingdom? Whose life will you enrich today? How do you want to be remembered? Want to be remembered as the one who was happy and joyful and always pointed out the silver lining even in the darkest situations? Or, do you want to be remembered as the serious, uptight, doom and gloom bringer of harsh reality? You decide, you get to make that choice every day.

Remember laughter is great medicine.

October 6

<u>Past</u>

Don't let your past define you. When you came to God he not only forgave you for your past, He forgot it. So why are you still letting it haunt you? Let the knowledge that you gained from that refine you and make you better, stronger. Other than that, remember the past is the past. You can't go back and do it again but we can learn from it and make the future different, better. It is not necessarily the beginning of a race that is as important as the end. Finish well, finish stronger.

"Brethren, I count not myself to have apprehended: but this one thing I do; forgetting those things which are behind, and reaching forth unto those things which are before. I press toward the mark for the prize of the high calling of God in Christ Jesus."- Philippians 3:13-14

October 7

<u>Not alone</u>

God is timeless. You might not see Him but he is there. Don't focus on what is seen, focus on the unseen. If you are stressed and struggling, remember God is always faithful. When your chest feels tight and it feels like the weight of the world is on your shoulders, take a breath and speak his name. Jesus. There is something about that name. Sometimes that is all that is needed. I love how when we need Him most is when He grows the closest to us. Everyone has their own path, true, but that doesn't mean that we have to walk it alone. God is always there.

"teaching them to observe all things whatsoever I have commanded you: and, lo, I am with you always even unto the end of the world. Amen"- Matthew 28:20

October 8

<u>No distance</u>

There is no distance that God can't cover to get to you. He will leave the 99 to come find you. It doesn't matter if it is dark and stormy or warm and sunny. Wherever you are he can rescue you. He loves you that much! You are highly favored. He thinks about you above all others. He created you. You are his masterpiece. He knows the number of hairs on your head. He has counted your tears. You are his Beloved.

Talk to him. It doesn't need to be some fancy words or eloquent speech, just share your heart. He knows already He is just waiting for you to ask.

"How think ye? If man have a hundred sheep, and one of them be gone astray, doth he not leave the ninety and nine, and goeth into the mountains, and seeketh that which is gone astray? And if so be that he find it, verily I say unto you, he rejoiceth more of that sheep, than of the ninety and nine which went not astray. Even so it is not the will of your Father which is in heaven, that one of these little ones should perish." Matthew 18:12-14

"Ye lust, and have not: ye kill, and desire to have, and cannot obtain: ye fight and war, yet ye have not, because ye ask not."- James 4:2

October 9

Difficulty

I have found that difficulty keeps me on track.

When things are hard, I depend on God more which in turn helps to strengthen my relationship with him.

My faith gets strengthened.

I think sometimes God allows things to happen that he knows will restore some things we have lost along the way. He shares with us the things that we need to hear. Whatever your circumstances are pray for understanding and he will give it to you.

October 10

Unspoken requests

God hears us sometimes when we say nothing at all with our lips. He hears our heart. I think sometimes in our brokenness he understands our groaning. But we are also to call out to him even if nothing makes it out. He wants it all. He wants the ugly and the messy. There is no need for you to clean it up for Him. He knows your heart.

God is good and does good.

"For my thoughts are not your thoughts, neither are your ways my ways, saith the Lord. For as the heavens are higher than the earth, so are my ways higher than your ways, and my thoughts than your thoughts." - Isaiah 55:8-9

October 11

Sentimental

I am very sentimental. I feel things very deeply. I love things that speak to my heart. I love things with sentimental value. The price tag really doesn't matter to me. It's all about the personal meaning. This creates such a happy emotion for me. Closeness if you might. I can't help but feel that God created emotions to help us connect with one another and Him. Now I am not saying let your emotions decide and dictate everything you do but allowing yourself to feel emotions can help you grow closer to others.

"But you, Lord are a compassionate and gracious God, slow to anger, abounding in love and faithfulness."- Psalm 86:15

October 12

He knows

God knows you. He calls you by your name. He values you and wants to bless you with good things. All of God's promises and his word are true. Isn't it nice to know that God never changes? That the God from the bible is still the God we have relationship with today. God will not force himself on you. He leaves the decision up to you. But he promises that if you choose Him he will stay with you.

"Abide in me, and I in you. As the branch cannot bear fruit of itself, except it abide in the vine; no more can ye, except ye abide in me. I am the vine, ye are the branches: He that abideth in me, and I in him, the same bringeth forth much fruit: for without me ye can do nothing. "- John 15:4-5

October 13

<u>Vindication</u>

Let's be honest with ourselves. At times, we all have hoped that folks would get what is coming to them. That person that speeds past us secretly (and sometimes not secretly at all) we hope that an officer is just around the corner. Or we hope that that person at work that does more slacking off than working finally gets caught. We should all be so glad that God is not like we are. God sent his son to die for us to save us from our sins while we were yet sinners. As he was going to the cross we were cruel and hateful and showed no mercy or compassion. I am so very glad that God didn't give me what I deserve. I am glad that he showed mercy and grace. Remember the devil is a liar and an accuser. I am not saying that bad deeds shouldn't be dealt with but having an ounce of compassion goes a long way.

"Judge not, that ye be not judged."- Matthew 7:1

"Dearly beloved, avenge not yourselves, but rather give place unto wrath: for it is written, vengeance is mine; I will repay, saith the Lord. Therefore if thine enemy hunger, feed him; if he thirst, give him drink: for in so doing thou shalt heap coals of fire on his head."- Romans 12:19-21

October 14

<u>Social Media</u>

Not all interaction on social media is bad. There are several positives to social media. I like to keep up with my family and friends. I try to be positive and share encouraging posts and share information about Jesus or church activities that I hope can help bless someone's day. A person can read and learn about almost anything they can think of with just a few strokes on a keyboard. However, there are certain aspects of social media that are toxic. All the negativity and all the belittling posts are toxic and breed only hate and discord. If you are using it to judge or measure your life against someone else's it does more harm than good. Make sure that you know when enough is enough. If you are not spending time with your family and instead are only living your life out on line, one day you will wake up and find out that you are all alone. What good is thousands or even millions of followers if you are ultimately alone? Be present with the real people in your life.

October 15

Set apart

As followers of Christ we are called to be a people set apart and distinct. Why would God need us to be exactly like everyone else? He wants you to be sanctified. You have been set apart from being in bondage to sin. You no longer need to fear death. You are to live for God and do it openly and wholeheartedly. Not only should your public life revolve around God but your private life as well. Your private life should be spent in prayer and in the word of God, not because it is required but because it is necessary for the power of your public life for Him.

"You have been set apart as holy to the Lord your God, and he has chosen you from all the nations of the earth to be his own special treasure."

Deuteronomy 14:2

October 16

<u>Distracted</u>

At times we can all become distracted and lose site of the ultimate goal.

But if we are wise, we can get closer to God to get more connected. Remember in our weakness, He is made strong. Our weakness is a platform for God's strength to be magnified.

Pray. Even Jesus knew how important it was to pray.

"And in the morning, rising up a great while before day, he went out, and departed into a solitary place, and there prayed." - Mark 1:35

October 17

<u>What you have</u>

What if I told you that God created you with everything you would need to succeed for him? You only need to use what you have. Treasure that quirk or skill that only you have. The thing that makes you different that separates you from the rest is your gift.

The enemy knows if he can only trick you into believing you are not enough, he knows you will never begin. If you never begin, then he won't have to stop you. What you have is enough. You are enough; and that frightens the enemy. If you only knew your worth in your Creator you would be unstoppable!

"Every good gift and every perfect gift is from above, and cometh down from the Father of lights, with whom is no variableness, neither shadow of turning."- James 1:17

October 18

I don't know.

These 3 words don't mean a lot to some folks. To me they are very special. My grandson is autistic and these words were the first sentence I ever heard him say. We were thrilled. We said it all the time. Repetition is the key, right? My Mom sent me a thing recently about the "I don't know prayer". Never heard of it? Neither had I, but when I read the article she sent me it made perfect sense. It was powerful even. One of the most powerful prayers that you can pray is these 3 simple words. There are a lot of times we don't know what to do, where to go, or what choices to make. But you are praying to the God who does know! And that prayer alone can make such a difference. Just admitting you have no idea and that you need His help. How powerful. I never realized exactly how powerful 3 little words could be. And like with my grandson's situation, repetition is the key. Pray it often. Every time you find yourself in a situation that you have no idea what or how or who? Pray, "I don't know." And give it to God. He knows. And God, who knows, can help navigate you through whatever situation you might be in.

October 19

God's word

Have you ever been walking at night when it is dark? It is scary to do too much maneuvering around without a flashlight or something to illuminate your path right? You never know what can be lurking in the dark. There could be a snake, or a giant whole or a cliff. There are so many things that can happen or go wrong. But when you have a light so you can see, it feels better right? You are more at ease because you can see.

God's word is a light.

Let that soak in for a minute. All those things that I talked about above, about how scary the unknown is without a light source to illuminate the way. Think about how much better you feel when you can see. Now think about God's word being a light. It illuminates your path shows you the way in the darkness! WOW.

"Thy word is a lamp unto my feet, and a light unto my path."- Psalm 119:105

October 20

No coincidences

I don't believe in coincidences.

I think things happen for a reason.

God has a plan.

I don't think we will understand it all until much later, maybe even heaven for some events but it's connected. God can use a thing that was meant for evil to bring good into our lives. We don't know what God knows. It is probably best that way. I'm not sure that we could handle the full plan. I think it would be too much and keep us from enjoying the here and now.

October 21

The plan

There is a plan for each of us. I think we truly start living the plan when we stop trying to figure it all out. Trust God for your future. Live on purpose, with a purpose. Know that it is not only about the destination but also about the journey. Your final destination is Heaven. But take one step at a time. Listen for God's voice. You don't have to figure it all out. He will be with you every step of the way. Every battle on the path, every position that you take, every mountain top and every valley it all is a part of your path home. Stop striving so much. Rest when you can. Begin again each day.

"Trust in the Lord with all thine heart; and lean not unto thine own understanding. In all thy ways acknowledge him, and he shall direct thy paths." Proverbs 3:5-6

October 22

In the living

Sometimes when we are asked how things are going we often say "Just living the dream." Whenever someone says that phrase to me, I often am left confused. Are they being sarcastic? Or are they really living out their dreams? It is very different when you are truly living out your dreams. Sometimes the dream changes from what it originally was. Sometimes what you might want is not what God intended for you to experience and he births in you a new dream. Sometimes the new dream is very different from your first expectation. Dreams do come true. Sometimes all God is waiting for is your surrender. Live with faith. Trust in His plan. And you might suddenly realize that what God intended for you is way better than what you had hoped.

"But without faith it is impossible to please him: for he that cometh to God must believe that he is, and that he is a rewarder of them that diligently seek him."- Hebrews 11:6

October 23

Adversity

Now wouldn't it be wonderful if we were never met with an adversity? What if things just always seemed to go your way? I feel like that would eventually lead to a very unsatisfactory life. Why you ask?

Well sometimes, it is in the hardship where we are tested and we can truly see what we are made of. We can also see who truly is a friend. When you are going through a rough patch, be sure to pay attention to those people cheering you on. Those are your people. You are not created to give up or throw in the towel at the first sign of difficulty. You come from a long line of over comers. Perseverance, dedication and devotion those are just some of the words to describe Christian people. You don't have to achieve salvation but you do have to receive it. Speak faith instead of doubt into your situation. Don't get quiet when you are threatened. Let God be the center of it all. Boldly speak of him and profess your faith.

"Now, Lord, consider their threats and enable your servants to speak your word with great boldness."- Acts 4:29

October 24

Desperate times

Ever heard that desperate times call for desperate measures? Well, sometimes God will use that desperation to push you. God knows we need a little push sometimes to make the changes. I am really bad about getting complacent. Even if I am in a place that is not necessarily the best for me, I can make it work. But is that really how God intended it to be? I don't believe so. He wants to move us but sometimes the only way those doors will open is when we are desperate.

God doesn't want you to stay unfulfilled. He wants you to get your miracle; even if that means that he has to shake things up to wake you up. Read below about the Canaan woman and her desperation. Would you have given up and walked away or would you have persisted like she did and received her miracle?

"And Behold, a woman of Canaan came out of the same coasts, and cried unto him, saying Have Mercy on me, O Lord, thou son of David; my daughter is grievously vexed with a devil. But he answered her not a word. And his disciples came and besought him, saying; Send her away; for she cried after us. But he answered and said, I am not sent but unto the lost sheep of the house of Israel. Then came and she worshipped him saying Lord, help me. But he answered and said it is not meet to take the children's bread, and cast it to the dogs. And she said, truth, Lord: yet the dogs eat of the crumbs which fall from their masters' table. Then Jesus answered and said unto her, o Woman, great is thy faith: be it unto thee even as thou wilt. And her daughter was made whole from that very hour. "- Matthew 15:22-28

October 25

Solitude

Two people can look at this word with very different feelings. One can see alone as being refreshing and wonderful, while another can see it as lonely and a very desolate place. I guess it all depends on your perspective.

I enjoy alone time. I am an only child and I am okay and comfortable being alone. Sometimes I even crave it. Not that I don't love my family and friends and enjoy spending time with them, but I also need time alone with my Heavenly Father. It replenishes me. It centers me and gets me ready to be out there again.

Jesus understood. He needed solitude too.

"And when he had sent the multitudes away, he went up into a mountain apart to pray: and when the evening was come, he was there alone."- Matthew 14:23

October 26

Intentional

No one has a great marriage by mistake. It takes work. You think of the other person, you care about their feelings, you build them up and want the best for them and in turn it makes you stronger together.

It is the same thing with being a Christian. No one accidently becomes a Christian. It is a conscience choice.

Be intentional with your decisions.

Plan it out. Make time for you to be alone with your creator. The Holy Spirit has so much to say. Not to condemn you but to strengthen you.

Get out your calendar and make a plan today. And stick with it as you would any important appointment.

October 27

Read the word

Whether you have one of the apps that help you to read the bible in a year or you are doing your own thing, make sure that you are in His word.

It is powerful and can tell you exactly what you need in a specific moment.

Listen to what God speaks to you.

"Because he hath set his love upon me, therefore will I deliver him: I will set him on high, because he hath known my name,"- Psalm 91:14

October 28

Anger

The Bible speaks about it. We have all felt it. I think certain things should make us angry such as injustice or crime. It's what we do with the anger that can be bad. In Ephesians, what the "let not the sun go down upon your wrath" means to me is don't hold on to it. Get angry; fix the issues if you can. If you can't fix the issues, use the knowledge that made you angry to change things, but then move on. Let it go. Don't let the anger consume you. Let the anger propel you to do something about the problem.

"Be ye angry, and sin not: let not the sun go down upon your wrath:" Ephesians 4:26

"Let every person be quick to hear, slow to speak, slow to anger; for the anger of man does not produce the righteousness of God." - James 1:19-20 ESV

October 29

Pray over your home

Do you pray over your home?

Your home should be your sanctuary.

Pray that all who enter your home feels love and leaves refreshed. Pray that your kids love their space and feel safe and protected. Pray for your spouse that he also views his home as a sanctuary and can't wait to come home. Pray that you aren't looking for perfection inside these walls.

Create an atmosphere of being present for your family.

October 30

Grateful heart

Begin each day with a grateful heart. Spend time daily in devotional time and prayer time with your creator. Speak love and kindness to those that you encounter.

"Rejoice always, pray continually, give thanks in all circumstances; for this is God's will for you in Christ Jesus."- 1 Thessalonians 5:16-18

Also read:

Psalm 28:7

Ephesians 5:20

October 31

Remember

Why is it so easy to remember the things we should forget and forget what we should remember?

The mind is confusing at best.

There are certain things that are stuck in my mind and no matter how hard I try they won't leave but that password I reset yesterday slips my mind.

The ways God always come through for me is not always the first thing I think of when I have an issue. I have a journal that I write down the miracles in so that I can pull that out and be reminded when I need it.

November 1

Spiritual battles

Spiritual battles are happening, all around you all the time. Some you have no idea about he waits for the perfect moment of weakness to strike. Some you can feel the effects of such as worry, stress, and fatigue. Sometimes the devil is busy keeping you distracted trying to figure these things out so he can take your peace. If he can keep you distracted enough from getting in the word of God, or praying or praising or worshipping he thinks he is closer to winning. The good news is we are on the winning team. Jesus already defeated the devil on the cross. Stand firm in your fight. God is always there to help you. Don't listen to the lies of the enemy.

November 2

Hunger

Ever been so very hungry? It was all you could think about right? Have you been spiritually hungry? Is your soul malnourished? Do you hunger for something deeper? Food won't fill this void. It can only be filled by getting into the word of God. When you are in the word of God reading and studying, when the enemy comes for you, you are ready. The word of God is like a sword. It helps defeat the enemy.

"But he answered and said , it is written, Man shall not live by bread alone, but by every word that proceedeth out of the mouth of God."- Matthew 4:4

"For the word of God is quick, and powerful, and sharper than any twoedged sword, piercing even to the dividing asunder of soul and spirit, and of the joints and marrows, and is a discerner of the thoughts and intents of the heart."- Hebrews 4:12

November 3

Communication

Communication is so important in any relationship.

It's the glue that keeps it all together.

That is why prayer is so very important in the Christian life.

Talk to God like you would talk to a friend.

November 4

Loneliness

People can be lonely for many reasons. Some is from loss of a spouse or loved one, others because of divorce or separation and others from poor decisions and choices that left them alone. Whatever the reason for the loneliness, it is real. You can do some simple things to help. You can join a support group. Sometimes simply removing yourself from social media can help to fix some of the issues. Self care and addressing any mental health issues can also benefit. Volunteering at a shelter or a soup kitchen can also boost your spirits and eliminate some feelings of loneliness.

Read the scriptures below :

Psalm 34:18

Isaiah 41:13

Mark 10:29-30

November 5

Joyful

Be Joyful always. Rejoice in the everyday things. Enjoy every moment of your life.

Don't be afraid of problems sometimes they are blessings in disguise. They are opportunities to bring you closer to God. When you wake in the morning, decide to be happy. Fix your thoughts on the good things in the day. Notice and appreciate your blessings.

Rejoice in the Lord always: and again I say, Rejoice. - Philippians 4:4

November 6

<u>Blessings</u>

Sometimes Blessings come in the form of pain and trouble (and as a friend at work said" The Lord is using this to teach you something") what an exciting thing to think about. His ways are greater than my ways. What good will come from this trouble?

God can calm all your fears and all your anxious thoughts, but you gotta trust Him.

To the world, enough will never be enough, but to God you alone are enough!

November 7

<u>OK to not Be OK</u>

It is perfectly fine to not be okay all the time.

No one is.

We all have off days.

On these not so perfect days we simply remember that better days are coming.

"You haven't seen all that God has n store for you; the best indeed is yet to come …"1 Corinthians 2:9

November 8

Thankful

Aren't you Glad that God doesn't stop being God when the situation is bad? Sometimes we are put in situations that are humbling to say the least.

In these situations, you learn more about yourself and your inner joy.

There is a peace that comes from Jesus that is not based on situations or circumstances.

"And the peace of God, which passeth all understanding, shall keep your hearts and minds through Christ Jesus. "- Philippians 4:7

November 9

Love of Jesus

Aren't you amazed at times at how Jesus loves you? He will never leave you. He won't betray you; he won't take advantage of you. He is your safe place and your confidant. He will never lie to you. Oh if we could only be this sure with all the loves in our life.

Ephesians 2:4

November 10

Goodness of God

Aren't you glad that God never gave up on you? Aren't you glad that those times when he was the last thing on your mind that he stood close by even when you kept pushing him away? He loved you so much he couldn't bear to be away from you.

In my life I have turned my back on him a few times but God never left me or forsake me. He received me back with open arms. I am so very thankful for his faithfulness.

November 11

Trust God

You can trust God with your problems. Lay them down with him and carry them no longer. Let him take your burdens away and rest. He longs for you to trust him enough to give them to him.

Psalm 68:19-20

Matthew 11:29-30

November 12

Tears

When I really stop and think about the love of Jesus, and how he went through all that he did for me it is overwhelming to my heart. Sometimes whether in church or in my car listening to worship music I am brought to tears (sometimes even sobbing).

November 13

What we need

God knows what we need.

I love that Jesus used parables for a lot of his teaching. He is such a good teacher making things relatable for us. He says things in a way so they resonate with us. It makes them more memorable. He understands us. He didn't have to come to this earth and live as a man. I believe he did this so that we could have an example; he left us with something to strive for.

November 14

God's timeline

God's timeline is not necessarily the same as ours.

But His plans are always better.

It is so very easy for us to forget all our blessings and all the times that God has come through for us. Our human minds only tend to remember the troubles. We forget all the times when God provided when there was no other way. I suggest you start a journal of all the times God showed up for you. It will help you remember. We all need to be reminded. In the Bible God commanded the Israelites to cross the Jordan River which he stopped miraculously and then after they crossed He told Joshua to take a member from each tribe to grab a stone and lay them down so that when future generations asked , they would remember what God had done for them. He knew how easily it is for us to forget.

I would suggest you read Joshua 4:1-8 for the full story of the 12 stones of remembrance.

Exodus 14:14 The Lord shall fight for you, and ye shall hold your peace.

November 15

Faith

Ever seen a mustard seed? It's small. It seems insignificant. I think it proves just how powerful faith is. The tiniest amount can do mighty things.

I love how Jesus uses parables to help us understand. He says things in a way so they resonate with us. It makes them more memorable.

"Jesus said unto him If thou canst believe, all things are possible to him that believeth"- Mark 9:23

November 16

Friends

God gives us friends so we don't have to go through this life alone. You need one. We hold each other up when we get weak.

The paralytic man's 4 friends in Mark 2:1-5 who brought him to Jesus is the ultimate friend goal.

Are your friends willing to get you to Jesus no matter what or how? We should all be so lucky to have friends like this.

These friends didn't care about conventional ways; they had to get their friend to Jesus. They knew if they could just get him to Jesus, even if it meant dropping him through the ceiling, they knew Jesus would heal him.

Matthew 9:1-8

Luke 5:17-26

November 17

God's plan for you

God has a mission specific for you. There is no backup plan. No pinch hitters. Only you can do what He has in mind for you to do. Do you know what your mission is? If not, might I suggest quiet time set aside for just you and God? Listen. God is speaking. It is up to us to hear what He is saying to us. Time alone in His presence is what allows us to hear Him more closely.

"A man's heart deviseth his way: but the Lord directeth his steps"- Proverbs 16:9

November 18

Who you are

Jesus is real.

He lives in my heart.

He helps me.

Some days he is the only thing getting me through the day.

He is faithful.

He wants to forgive all your sins and redeem you.

He is good and he does good.

November 19

<u>Stillness</u>

Science tells us that stillness regenerates our brains. Silence relieves stress and tension and helps us to gain perspective.

I think this might be once that the Bible and science agree. Being still is powerful! I would challenge you to just pick a time of the day that works best for you and just be still. Use this time to go into God's word and really listen. Not thinking about the things on your list for the day. Not wondering what you will make for breakfast or dinner. Just be still in His presence. It will make your "to do" list a lot more do-able

"Be still, and know that I am God: I will be exalted among the heathen, I will be exalted in the earth." - Psalms 46:10

November 20

<u>Desires</u>

Sometimes God puts desires in our heart. We need to stay close to God by prayer and by daily Bible study.

Sometimes what God asks us to do is not necessarily something we wanted to do, but if God brings you to it he will get you through it.

"Delight yourself in the Lord and he will give you the desires of your heart."- Psalm 37:4

November 21

Birthdays

Today is my birthday. The older I get the closer together they seem to come. I do love birthdays though. There is something about having your own special day. I always feel very loved and blessed.

"For we are his workmanship, created in Christ Jesus unto good works, which God hath before ordained that we should walk in them."- Ephesians 2:10

"Thou crownest the year with thy goodness; and thy paths drop fatness."

Psalm 65:11

November 22

Shepherd

Sheep don't fear their shepherd. He protects them. He keeps them safe and looks after them. If one of them goes astray he leaves the group and goes to get it. How wonderful to have a caretaker that loves you this much.

We are his sheep.

"My sheep hear my voice, and I know them and they follow me: And I give unto them eternal life; and they shall never perish, neither shall any man pluck them out of my hand."- John 10:27-28

November 23

<u>Finish big</u>

It's the little things that determine the big things.

Don't underestimate small beginnings. Just because you start small doesn't mean you can't finish big!

Let God's peace help you to eliminate fear in your daily life.

"Thou has been faithful over a few things, I will make thee ruler over many things: enter thou into the joy of the Lord" Matthew 25:21

November 24

<u>Big God</u>

It's easy to forget how much we depend on God when our day is going smoothly. Throw in a traffic jam, a few mishaps at work and all of sudden we are back to seeing how we need God every minute of every day.

What I have learned is that in the tough times is when I have walked closer to God. I see just how small I am. God shows up in those moments in a big way and suddenly all my problems feel smaller.

The Lord God is my strength, and he will make my feet like hinds' feet, and he will make me walk upon mine high places. To the chief singer on my stringed instruments. - Habakkuk 3:19

November 25

<u>Not a Secret</u>

Are you doing your part to "draw others out of the darkness"? Why is it so hard for us to share about God's love with others? If Chic-fil-a were giving away free food, we would tell EVERYONE; because, we don't want them to miss out right? Well it's the same with God's love! I know some days it is the only thing holding me together. Share your faith with those close to you. Your love for God shouldn't be a secret.

Let's not keep something so valuable away from our loved ones.

"May you experience the love of Christ, though it is too great to understand fully. Then you will be made complete with all the fullness of life and power that comes from God."- Ephesians 3:19 NLT

"Happy are those who hear the joyful call to worship, for they will walk in the light of your Presence, Lord. They exult in your righteousness."- Psalm 89:15-16

November 26

<u>Help</u>

There will always be problems in this world.

If you make sure your focus is on Jesus you will have less time to focus on your problems.

We were created to look at and to God for your source of help.

"In everything give thanks: for this is the will of God in Christ Jesus concerning you"- 1 Thessalonians 5:18

"My help cometh from the Lord, which made heaven and earth"- Psalm 121:2

November 27

Gone

God doesn't remember our sins. Why do you keep rehashing and beating yourself up for them? The moment that you trusted Jesus Christ as your Lord and Savior you were wrapped in Christ's righteousness. Clothes in white, covered with his love and his blood that He shed for us all.

"As far as the east is from the west, so far hath He removed our transgressions from us."- Psalm 103:12

*I think it is described to us this way so our finite minds can comprehend the gravity of them truly being removed.

"But God commendeth his love toward us in that, while we were yet sinners, Christ died for us. Much more then, being now justified by his blood, we shall be saved from wrath through him." -Romans 5:8-9

November 28

One day at a time

There is time for everything. Slow down and enjoy it. Make a habit of enjoying everything.

Don't rush through one event to get to another. Before you know it, your children are grown and married and you are nearing retirement and it's the end of your life.

Remember no season lasts forever whether it is a good season or a bad season. So enjoy the good and know that the bad won't last forever.

There is a time for everything and a season for every activity under the heavens-Ecclesiastes 3:1

November 29

Believe

Are you troubled?

Why?

God's word is true.

His promises are true.

He can't lie.

Trust in him and his promises.

"Let not your heart be troubled; ye believe in God, believe also in me. In my father's house are many mansions: if it were not so, I would have told you. I go to prepare a place for you. And if I go to prepare a place for you I will come again, and receive you unto myself; that where I am, there ye may be also" - John 14:1-3

November 30

Diversions

Sometimes our direction of travel gets diverted. This can happen literally and figuratively.

I remember back to a church trip that we were on. There were a couple of vans traveling together. The person driving the van that I was in knew the way there. But our driver took the wrong road and I remember he was very surprised and joking around with the other van driver that he had missed his turn and we turned around at a new station parking lot and headed back to our correct road. What we didn't know at that moment was that there was a HUGE wreck that had taken place and had he taken the correct road, we would have been right there and probably involved in it as well. That has always stuck with me.

Sometimes God uses detours to get us safely to our destinations. These detours are not always convenient and sometimes we don't understand. Sometimes we are upset at the delay not knowing what we are being protected from.

"For he shall give his angels charge over thee, to keep thee in all thy ways. They shall bear thee up in their hands, lest thou dash thy foot against a stone." - Psalms 91: 11-12

December 1

Carpenter

To think about the Son of God and how he could have been anything but chose to be a carpenter, got me to thinking. He came as a man, and chose a job where he was building and creating with a man's hands. There is something special about creating and building things.

"Is not this the carpenter son of Mary, Brother of James and Joses and Judas and Simon and are not his sisters here with us? And they took offenses at him."

Mark 6:3

December 2

Gardening

I acquired my love of gardening from my father. Gardening for him was a labor of love. Dad never complained about all the hard work of gardening. He truly enjoyed all of it. Gardening is a form of therapy and relaxation for me. There is just something about watching your plants grow and produce. I think God feels this way about us. He references these many times in His word. He speaks about knowing them by their fruits. He speaks about being the vine. I feel like God totally gets my love of gardening because He is a gardener too. We are his crop.

"Ye shall know them by their fruits. Do men gather grapes of thorns, or figs of thistles? Even so every good tree bringeth forth good fruit but a corrupt tree bringeth forth evil fruit. A good tree cannot bring forth good fruit.Every tree that bringeth not forth good fruit is hewn down and cast into the fire. Wherefore by their fruits ye shall know them." - Matthew 7: 16-20

December 3

Yoked together

I was doing some reading and learned that 2 animals of different sizes and strengths shouldn't be yoked together because the smaller, weaker animal would be in constant pain and pressure.

Which got me to thinking- Jesus is stronger than I am but He promises that if we are yoked with him that the burden will be light.

I think it is saying that when we trust him fully that we are clothed in his righteousness and therefore he takes on all the heavy lifting.

We have all likely heard the scripture: "Come unto me, all ye that labour and are heavy laden, and I will give you rest. Take my yoke upon you, and learn of me; for I am meek and lowly in heart: and ye shall find rest unto your souls."- Matthew 11:28-29

"Be ye not unequally yoked together with unbelievers: for what fellowship hath righteousness with unrighteousness? And what communion hath light with darkness "- 2 Corinthians 6:14

December 4

The Journey

Life is not all about the destination but about the journey. Enjoy getting there. I always love car trips. Sometimes the conversations and what happens on the way there is my favorite part. Those talks and all the laughing and jokes are priceless to me. I don't mind a few extra hours in the car.

Being with the people in the car with me is exactly where I want to be anyway.

Don't look back and realize you were waiting to be happy until you got to your destination.

Be happy in the now.

Enjoy every day.

Enjoy every part of the journey.

December 5

<u>Marriage</u>

Marriage has always been sacred.

There is something so very special when you witness 2 people get it right. When you get to see them do it like God intended. It makes you feel good knowing that the vows that they took mean something.

God intended for Him to be the center of the marriage.

"Love is patient, love is kind. It does not boast. It is not proud. It does not dishonor others. It is not self-seeking. It is not easily angered. It keeps no record of wrongs. " -1 Corinthians 13:4-5

December 6

<u>Bless the World</u>

God will use you to bless others. Share all your blessings. God blesses us to be a blessing to others.

By the measure you give it will be given back to you.

And if you don't have anything to share, share a smile.

They are free.

They cost nothing but can change someone's day.

And by changing someone's day you just might change their life!

Luke 6:38-40

December 7

Happiness

Being grateful for all God is, is the beginning to happiness.

When you realize it's not about you, it takes a lot of worry and weight off of your shoulders.

None of us can ever be or do enough to earn God's love.

Thank God because of Jesus we are enough. He did what no human could ever do. Simply because He loves you!

"For God so loved the world that he gave his only begotten Son, that whosoever believeth in him should not perish, but have everlasting life." - John 3:16

"No eye has seen, no ear has heard, and no mind has imagined what God has prepared for those who love Him"- 1 Corinthians 2:9

December 8

<u>Eyes to see and ears to hear</u>

I pray often to have eyes that truly see and ears that hear.

Sometimes I think we miss a lot. Not intentionally. Sometimes we are too close to the issue. Other times, I think our own personal issues get in the way. This clouds our vision and stops us from hearing. I think when we pray for understanding we have to be prepared to truly listen and see those around us and their needs. If we truly want to be the hands and feet of Jesus we have to be concerned about the things that He is concerned about.

God loves people. He loves all people even with their messes and their issues.

"For the Son of man is come to seek and save that which is lost"- Luke 19: 10

"For God so loved the world, that he gave his only begotten Son, that whosoever believeth in him should not perish, but have everlasting life."- John 3:16

"But God commendeth his love toward us, in that, while we were yet sinners, Christ died for us. "- Romans 5:8

December 9

Those days that you are awakened at 2 AM, I think it is God wanting to wake you up to spend a little extra "alone time" with you.

In my experience looking back, those are the days that might be a little more difficult. They might be a little more challenging. He knows you might need that extra time in prayer.

Always bring glory to your creator in every situation. On those days you are awakened, go into prayer and ask the Lord to reveal what He has for you. And wait -

"Cause me to hear thy lovingkindness in the morning; For in thee do I trust: Cause me to know the way wherein I should walk; For I lift up my soul unto thee."- Psalm 143:8

December 10

Roots

Did you know that plants need to be repotted at least every 2 years so they don't get "pot-bound".

You see all the nutrients in the soil gets used up and even if the plant doesn't need more room to grow, it doesn't thrive anymore.

It happens to us too. Sometimes you need to loosen the soil around our souls, find something that sparks our imagination, quickens our pulse or just brings a smile to our faces.

You have to get yourself into some nutrient rich soil!

Psalm 18:16-19 MSG

December 11

Don't compare

Don't compare yourself to others. Their journey is not yours. And the same your journey is not theirs. God has a specific plan for you. He has equipped you for your journey. He hasn't equipped you for your friend's journey or your enemy for that matter. It is specific to you.

Don't let social media's highlight reels get you down. People usually only share the good stuff. That is not realistic. And definitely not worth losing any sleep over.

No one is perfect. Look at yourself the way Jesus does with love and grace.

"But unto every one of us is giving grace according to the measure of the gift of Christ."- Ephesians 4:7

December 12

<u>Ask</u>

Sometimes the most powerful thing you can do for a person is lift them up in prayer.

There are so many things that people are going through that we know nothing about. God knows.

If you see a friend struggling, pray for them. If you know they have had a bad week, pray for them. If you know they have had a good week, pray for them. Pray that it continues for them. See an ailment in their body pray for healing.

Jesus said that we would do even greater things. But we have to ask. Seek and you will find. Are you looking for miracles? Are you praying in expectation?

"Verily, verily, I say unto you, He that believeth on me, the works that I do shall he do also; and greater works than these shall he do; because I go unto my Father."- John 14:12

December 13

<u>A puzzle</u>

Ever been putting together a puzzle and as you get close to being finished you realize that you are missing a piece?

A single piece makes all the difference.

How disappointed and frustrating. Doing all that and still there is the void of the missing piece. Life is like that. You can get yourself together and try to do the best you can, but without that missing piece you aren't whole. God is that missing piece.

"God made my life complete when I placed all the pieces before him, When I got my act together, he gave me a fresh start. Now I'm alert to God's ways; I don't take God for Granted. Every day I review the ways he works; I try not to miss a trick. I feel put back together, and I'm watching my step. God wrote the text of my life when I opened the book of my heart to his eyes. "-Psalm 18: 20-24

December 14

<u>Speak Life</u>

Choose the people very carefully that are in your circle. Bad company can corrupt good character. Choose to spend your time around life giving people. Spend your time around people that speak positive things over you and encourage you to be better. They say you can know your future by looking at the five people closest to you.

1 Corinthians 15:33

December 15

<u>Only human</u>

Have you ever just stopped to think about the human body? Are you amazed at how God thought of everything? I am so amazed thinking about everything from a yawn to a hiccup, all the organs and veins and all their functions and how everything has its own purpose. Just think about the complexity of all the inner working of your body. Think about all the things that work together in such a way so that you are you. You are so complex. God created all of that and yet he knows you so well that he knows exactly how many hairs are on your head. It amazes me at how complex and yet how personal.

"Thank you for making me so wonderfully complex! Your workmanship is marvelous- and how well I know it." Psalm 139:14

"But even the very hairs of your head are all numbered. Fear not therefore: ye are more valuable than many sparrows." - Luke 12:7

December 16

<u>God's ways</u>

Usually if you ask me a question and I really don't know why something happened, my standard response is "God's Ways are greater than my ways". It's true. Sometimes we will not understand why something happened the way it did. All I know is God can turn what was meant for evil into good. He knows all and is over all.

I don't know the reasons, but I do trust His plans.

"And we know that all things work together for good to them that love God, to them who are called according to his purpose"- Romans 8:28

December 17

<u>Church</u>

I love my church. When I go there I get refilled and refreshed every time.

God speaks to me through the messages and the songs.

I love to hear just the voices when we sing the song " I exalt thee". I love to see all the hands raised in worship service. Sometimes I imagine how God must feel being showed all that praise. It makes me smile, sometimes it makes me cry.

I feel so many emotions.

I would hope that you also have a place where you get to experience this. It is amazing to be a part of praise and worship service.

There is really nothing else like it.

You don't NEED to go to church to go to Heaven, but why wouldn't you want to? If the church body is going to be the folks with you in Heaven, why not start getting used to them.

Don't go for any other reason than to meet with and hear from God; and you won't be disappointed.

December 18

<u>Names of God</u>

God has many names. They all mean so many different things. But He is one in the same. He is the Lord God almighty, our healer, our provider and our protector.

Yahweh- Lord, Jehovah

Jehovah Rapha- The Lord that heals

Jehovah Jireh- The Lord our Provider

El Shaddai- Lord God Almighty

Elohim- God

Elohim Shomri- God is my protector

"I am the Lord thy God, which have brought thee out of the land of Egypt, out of the house of bondage. "- Exodus 20:2

December 19

<u>Satan</u>

Satan tries to accuse us. He is happiest when he is heaping feelings of guilt upon us. As believers, he wants us covered with feelings of guilt. It's easier to shame us. All of this is intended to keep you from having joy. It is all to encourage you to doubt God and His wisdom. We wont understand a lot of things that happen in this world. And that is ok as long as we remember that God is good and He does good. The devil is a liar.

Remember Satan is a liar and the father of Lies- John 8:44

"Be sober, be vigilant; because your adversary the devil, as a roaring lion, walketh about, seeking whom he my devour."- 1 Peter 5:8

December 20

Perfection

God knew that we would never be perfect in this life so he sent Jesus. Don't think that everything (including you) needs to be perfect for you to be happy. It won't ever happen.

I'm glad God doesn't require perfection he just wants surrender and progress.

"When the perfect comes, the partial will be done away"- 1 Corinthians 13:10

December 21

Mindset

How many of us have something happen and we get all in our "feels" and let it define our day? I do. Matter of fact I did this just yesterday. I got a big project at work (a couple actually) -no problem. I love to be busy. Then one thing after another happens and BOOM! I'm in my own little pity party. Shame on me!

Instead of focusing on the current set of circumstances or problems, stop and see the big picture.

I am a child of GOD. I am loved by the most High.

I decide how I react to issues.

I have been forgiven of it all. It is well with my soul.

Don't let silly circumstances or a tainted mindset rob you of your joy. Every day is precious.

We all have loved ones not here with us. If we won't do it for ourselves, let's do it for them. LIVE, joyously and to the fullest.

"May the Lord of peace Himself give you peace at all times and in every way."-   2 Thessalonians 3:16

December 22

Bold

I thank God that we can have a gentle quiet spirit and still have a bold personality. God made you the way you are for a reason.

"Humble yourselves before the Lord and he will lift you up"- James 4:10

"Rather it should be that of your inner self, the unfading beauty of a gentle and quiet spirit which is of great worth in God's sight"- 1 Peter 3:4

December 23

Only one you

Live the life God has for you.

Everyone is on a different journey.

God will equip you with what you need.

Be thankful and grateful for the people in your life. You were created unique for your mission. There are several people whose lives are happier just because you are in it. Think of the people that you feel better just being around; those folks who encourage and inspire you.

Who can you encourage and make happier?

Be the reason someone doesn't give up!

December 24

Sight

Have you ever been walking at night when it is dark?

It is scary to do too much maneuvering around without a flashlight or something to illuminate your path right?

You never know what can be lurking in the dark. There could be a snake, or a giant whole or a cliff. There are so many things that can happen or go wrong.

But when you have a light so you can see, it feels better right? You are more at ease because you can see.

God's word is a light.

Let that soak in for a minute; all those things that I talked about above; about how scary the unknown is without a light source to illuminate the way. Think about how much better you feel when you can see.

Now think about God's word being a light. It illuminates your path shows you the way in the darkness!

WOW.

"Thy word is a lamp unto my feet, and a light unto my path."- Psalm 119:105

December 25

Jesus

It is Jesus Birthday today! Celebrate Him!

For all he did for the world!

"For unto us a child is born, unto us a son is given: and the government shall be upon his shoulder: and his name shall be called Wonderful, Counselor, The mighty God, The everlasting Father, The Prince of Peace."- Isaiah 9:6

December 26

Memories

I love to look back on old pictures or I love the memories on Face book that pop up and remind me of things that I have forgotten. I love to be reminded of things that my little one said long ago or did. I was reminded this morning that I forgot because I am human. I can usually remember the things I did wrong or my mistakes like they were yesterday- But God forgets our mistakes and our not so great moments cause he forgives us. As far as the east is from the west so are our transgressions.

Psalm 103:12

December 27

Not the right time

I was thinking.

Some things only will work out if you wait.

While planning a party I was thinking of all the to and that had to be done; invitations, party supplies, calling the caterer, ordering the cake- But some things have to wait till the day of the party- for us it's decorating and buying that salad mix- yes it needs to be done but the timing has to be right-Man this was so insightful for me: a list maker and an impatient person.

I want God to do everything NOW- all at once- right away and he is whispering to me this morning- that bagged salad won't last- it's not time yet- but the time is coming- Soon!

Be patient, all in His time.

December 28

Pray

We should pray without ceasing. If we prayed as much as we worried, the world would be such a better place.

"Be careful for nothing; but in everything by prayer and supplication with thanksgiving let your requests be made known unto God. And the peace of God, which passeth all understanding, shall keep your hearts and minds through Christ Jesus."

December 29

Let Go and Let God

Sometimes all our human efforts end up like a train wreck. We won't always get it all right- even when we have the best of intentions.

"That's why I take pleasure in my weaknesses and in the insults, hardships, persecutions, and troubles that I suffer for Christ. For when I am weak, then I am strong." - 2 Corinthians 12:10 NLT

December 30

Grace

Sometimes we are broken, but we are not trash. God uses our weakness to emphasize His strength.

"For by grace are ye saved through faith; and not of yourselves: it is the gift of God: Not of works, lest any man should boast. For we are his workmanship, created in Christ Jesus unto good works, which God hath before ordained that we should walk in them. " - Ephesians 2:8-9

December 31

Recharge your batteries

We all have those moments to where we feel like we can't go on. I would encourage you to take time for you. Get away from it all. Recharge your batteries. You can't pour from an empty cup.

Think about where your strength comes from. Get back to your relationship with your creator.

When you truly get back to the basics, the rest is so much better.

"But they that wait upon the Lord shall renew their strength; they shall mount up with wings as eagles; they shall run, and not be weary; and they shall walk, and not faint."- Isaiah 40:31

www.ingramcontent.com/pod-product-compliance
Lightning Source LLC
Chambersburg PA
CBHW071327120626
46546CB00002B/476